WITHDRAWN

REFORM OF THE CHURCH

REFORM OF THE CHURCH

*Crisis and Criticism
in Historical Perspective*

ROBERT E. McNALLY, S.J.

HERDER AND HERDER

1963
HERDER AND HERDER NEW YORK
232 Madison Avenue, New York 16, N.Y.

Imprimi potest: John J. McGinty, S.J.
                  Praep. Prov. Neo Eboracensis

Nihil obstat: Patrick A. Barry
                  Censor deputatus

Imprimatur: † Robert F. Joyce
              Bishop of Burlington
              July 16, 1963

CONTENTS

CONTENTS

FOREWORD

The Church of Christ as the Christian believer sees her through the eyes of faith is a reality beautiful and fair. Her eschatological appearance will be without spot or wrinkle (Eph. 6:27). Yet until Christ comes again, she looks more like the tired old woman seen by Hermas in his vision (*The Shepherd of Hermas*, Vis. 10–11). The defects of the Church in every time are visible to friend and foe alike. These defects repel the foe and make the friend sad. Those who love her wish to wash the grime away and this manifests the perpetual nisus to reform within the Church. We find it in Paul's letters and in the Johannine writings. Hermas himself manifests it. In the late Middle Ages the cry was for the reform of the Church "in head and members." We also speak of the Reform and the counter-reform. Perhaps this latter term is not exact. In the sixteenth century there were two reform movements: one operated from outside of the traditional framework of ecclesiastical life, and the other worked from within it. The first brought forth the Protestant communities and the second ushered in the Post-Tridentine phase of Roman Catholicism.

The ecumenical movement is an attempt to reconcile the two reforms irenically. The conflict of the two reforms brought about separation and separation is an evil which the ecumenist wishes to overcome. Certainly one of the facets of the Second Vatican Council is professedly ecumenical, and much of the drive for Church reform makes itself palpable in conciliar circles.

We certainly need to reflect on the different elements which entered into the complicated phenomenon of the sixteenth-century reforms. The historian must help us in our need. In the past such history was given, but in a partisan spirit. Our current historians are anxious to avoid such an approach to the facts of yesterday. Many more facts have been discovered in recent times, giving us the possibility to see a fuller picture of the tragic moment behind us. Of course, we do not expect that a contemporaneous writer will be completely free from all partisan spirit. It is nonetheless gratifying to know that impartiality is the ideal goal toward which he strives, even though his very humanity condemns him to fail somewhat in his pursuit.

The present essay by Dr. Robert McNally, S.J., is an offering, especially to Catholics, to see the sixteenth-century ecclesiastical reality in its roots. He is not engaged in polemics. He is a Roman Catholic and his loyalties will give his study an indeliberate slant to his Church's advantage. However, it is obvious that he is also ecumenically minded. His rapid pulling together of the various factors in the historical complex, now called the Reformation, should help all those who are striving to bring the different Christian communities into fruitful and fraternal conversation in the dynamic hope for unity.

Father McNally's study supposes the massive work of many predecessors. As a tight concentration of voluminous matter it is a kindness to the ecumenists of our day. If it serves them in their work, the book will have achieved its purpose.

GUSTAVE WEIGEL, S.J.

INTRODUCTION

"The need of Church reform," wrote Johannes Haller, "is verifiable through many centuries and is perhaps as old as the Church itself." For the Church on earth reflects the tribulation of God's chosen people in the wilderness, their loyalty and devotion to Him as well as their infidelity and apostasy, their constant need to be reminded from on high of their holy vocation. The Church of history throbs with anguish and concern for the spiritual well-being of her members; in the midst of contemporary decadence it is her tireless struggle to preserve her supernatural character and to remain faithful to her exalted redemptive mission. Throughout the centuries she has been absorbed in the task of narrowing the gap between the noble profession of the Christian faith and its poor fulfillment, between the high aspiration to sanctity and its meager realization. The burden of leading fallen humanity to that blessed life which the Saviour promises is not an easy one, for the Christian while surrounded on all sides by the City of Man must think and love as a member of God's own City. And it is this tension that forms the crucial moment of Christian life. The

Church must "be to the world what the soul is to the body," a source of life and energy, through her poor human members who strive to live outwardly the faith of Christ which they profess inwardly.

When confronted with human weakness the Church is invariably realistic. For in the meaningful experience of her long history she has well learned the truth of the Gospel parable that in God's Kingdom the wheat and cockle, the good and the bad, grow side by side. When, however, the Lord of the harvest will finally appear, the separation of the two classes is definitive; meanwhile it is her role to understand, comfort, strengthen, heal and instill hope in the hearts of all men both good and bad. The Church, therefore, has never felt herself to be a community of saints but rather an assembly of men marked with the wounds of fallen nature and, while open to the allurement of evil, striving with God's grace to reach their heavenly Fatherland.

In a sense the Church is both divine and human—divine in her soul, which is the Holy Spirit, human in her members clerical and lay, who make up the body of the Church. It is within the human element that the problem of reform arises, for men, as free agents, have the inner power of deviating from grace and truth. And it is this deviation or departure from the law of God or from right reason that creates in the supernatural and natural order that *deformatio* which only *reformatio* can set right. The more profound, the more widespread is this deformation, the greater the crisis in the Church, the more urgent then and drastic becomes the reformation. For in its ultimate analysis deformation is a disease which, if neglected, grows furiously, until it fills the whole body of the Church. But it is from the divine element, the indwelling Spirit, that reform must come. And, in this sense, the Church is rightly said to reform herself.

The true reformer is a saver of life, a healer of disease, a repairer of damage, a restorer of form, a renewer of spirit. He is not a bringer of death. Reform of the Church must be structured on an exact knowledge of the Church herself, a knowledge which rests on the distinction between the essential and the accidental, the timeless and the temporal. It must understand the profound difference between the Church as constituted by Christ, and the Church as conditioned by history; between dogma, the immutable doctrine of the Church, and theology, its interpretation in the course of history; between the high sanctity to which the Church invites all men and the daily life of the Church as it is known in history. A reformer who disregards these important distinctions is not a true reformer for his work will be concerned more with death than life.

Because reformation aims at the preservation or conservation of excellence (e.g., sanctifying grace) or the prosecution and attainment of an ideal (e.g., moral perfection), the reformer must also understand in terms of both theology and history those basic principles on which the Church was originally founded by Christ. It is not sufficient that the ecclesiastical administrator await revelations and inspirations of the Holy Spirit to inform him of the ways and means of reform. He must study, and be advised by *periti* who understand the objective pattern according to which the Church is shaped. It is a matter of record that there have been disastrous reforms in the history of the Church which have been launched apart from her authentic tradition and, therefore, from her best interests; and frequently true reforms have been impeded by self-interest and ignorance or motivated by personal taste and subjective feeling.

Reformation is only valid inasmuch as it rediscovers the authentic stream of Catholic tradition and unites with it. It may be that at this or that historical moment this precious channel of life is to be sought only by turning back; but it is also possible that it can be found by taking steps forward, by change, alteration and development. Reformation depends on those who have the charismatic insight to discern the direction in which the Church must move, if she hopes to recover, rehabilitate, renew herself. Apart from an extraordinary miracle, reformation is in the ultimate analysis the work of a myriad of Christians of good will working together under the guidance of the Holy Spirit in the glorious work of building the heavenly Jerusalem which is God's City on earth.

Ecclesiastical reformation is not uniquely rooted in moral decadence. The history of the Church shows that reformation may also be inspired by and proceed from the need of intellectual and cultural renewal. When sacred learning, which is vital to the full development of the Church's intellectual life, decays, crisis is prepared. Christianity cannot subsist for long on ignorance. For in addition to being a saving religion and a way of life it is also a wisdom, an intellectualism, whose explication depends on the community of scholars working in harmony with the Church. The effort of Charles the Great (d. 814) to restore learning and education in the Frankish empire after the dark days of the Merovingians is a conspicuous example of intellectual reformation. For Charles' reform program, conceived in terms of the needs of the Christian religion, was directed to the cultivation of letters in order that the sacred text of Scripture and the right understanding of the Catholic faith might be better secured. "For although correct conduct may be better than knowledge," he wrote, "nevertheless knowledge comes before conduct." The Carolingian reform of literary study led to a reform of sacred theology, biblical exegesis, divine worship and ultimately to a renaissance in many different areas of Catholic life. All this signified a step forward in the subsequent development of Western culture, and provided a veritable renewal of Christianity.

But apart from the crises which moral and intellectual decadence have occasioned in the course of history, *deformatio* can also be born from the Church's failure to take notice of shifts in the world-situation, especially in the contemporary, cultural environment. Considered from the point of view of Western history, the unbroken continuity of the Church from the days of Tiberius Caesar to our own days is indeed striking. She has witnessed—in fact presided at—the birth and death of innumerable phases of the history of culture. In the past one thousand nine hundred years civilization has dissolved and reformed more than once. Its thoughts, values, ideals and methods have undergone extensive development in directions which could never have been foreseen. More than half the world has been discovered since the Church was founded, and now man is preparing to conquer new planetary worlds. Through all the flux and change of history, the Church has been able by successfully integrating herself with new cultures and civilizations to preserve her own character and identity. It is to her credit that she has been able to survive whereas other institutions have not.

Like all institutions in this world the Church is subject to time and confined by space. It can be enriched or impoverished by both. She is indeed guided by the Holy Spirit, presided over by Christ, but served by men. In terms of the Gospel parables, which from an early date have been applied to her, the greatest responsibility which the Church must bear is constant vigilance against the carelessness of the hireling, against the rapacity of the wolf, against the subversion of the evil sower. All internal deformation in the Church is traceable to its human members, to those who have been unfaithful either to grace or to truth or to both. When in the course of history we find the Church in the throes of grave internal crisis, we also find this crisis reflected in the inner life of the individual Christian who has been neglected, scandalized or maltreated, or victimized through the weakness of his own fallen nature. When the individual members of the Church, one by one, have been transformed and restored to the image of God, the decisive victory of reformation is always carried. Thus the burden of reformation rests on all the members of the Church.

The theme of this short essay is the *Reform of the Church,* a problem in itself so vast that only a library of books could handle it adequately. It is not therefore our intention to be either complete or novel; it is rather to suggest questions to the reader by inviting him to gaze on a picture of a large segment of Church History. The picture is not complete in detail. In fact, the reader will note here and there that it has been either overexposed or under-exposed; but despite that technical deficiency I trust that the principal object—the Church in crisis—will be obscured neither by too much light nor by too much shadow. It is this Church, our beloved Church, whose persistent existence despite the vicissitudes of history is indeed a moral miracle, that most interests us. The more intelligence we have of her structure and history, her development through the ages, the better we can provide for her contemporary needs.

The span of history that stretches approximately two and one half centuries, from the pontificate of Boniface VIII (1294–1303) to that of Pius IV (1559–65) does not find an exact parallel at present, but it is filled with relevance for all who know how to read it. Our contemporary problems are in another area. We are not especially concerned today with general moral decadence, papal captivity, universal schism, Renaissance humanism, theological exhaustion or any of the various vexations which tormented the Church through these long centuries. The contemporary problem involves the maturation of the Church in the post-modern world, her free, healthy growth in accord with her own special character, the full realization of her great potentialities, her accommodation and adaptation to the best aspects of modern society, her awareness of the important role which she must play in the complicated affairs of men. In the course of her history the Church has often been retarded by

men with the mind of 'yesterday' who have tried to guide
her through the world of 'today,' by men who have wanted
to bring the Church back to the past, to an ideal age of gold.
But because the Church is a living society, she may indeed
recall the past and plan for the future, but she must always
live in the present.

Throughout these few pages I have briefly described certain significant situations in the history of the Late Middle
Ages which may prove instructive to us who today live in
the post-Reformation world. However painful, even dis-
tressing, these episodes may be, they must be reviewed in
order that the central issues of reform and reformation be
grasped in terms of history. The sad story of ecclesiastical
abuse and error in the past, far from being a source of scandal, is part of God's didactic plan to teach His Church humility and modesty, to convince her that her destiny rests
in His powerful Hands, and that it was His Spirit that led
her out of the wilderness. Thus Leo XIII could say with
sincerity, "We have no fear of the publication of documents."

In the hope that what is here set down may excite interest, I have added bibliographical notes for further reading and study. Readers, who will take the time to look more
deeply into the history of the Church in the tragic days before the Reformation, will have helped to realize my purpose in writing this book.

II

The Papacy (1294–1414)

The sudden death of Pope Nicholas IV (the Minorite Girolamo Masci) on Good Friday, April 4, 1292, marks an end-phase in the history of the medieval papacy. The perennial contest between *Imperium* and *Sacerdotium*, so characteristic of the previous two centuries of papal history, was indeed terminated; and with the disastrous fall of Acre to Islam (May 18, 1291) life went out of the crusade movement which the papacy had protected and nourished for centuries.[1] At this historical moment the Holy See was badly in need of a pope with the moral courage and intellectual ability to face the complicated series of crises which beset it on all sides: the dread menace of Islam, the proposed general council, the difficult matter of the Sicilian Vespers, the impending war between England and France, the affairs of Charles II and Philip the Fair, the anti-papalism

[1] Cf. F. Gregorovius, *History of the City of Rome in the Middle Ages* 5, 2 (London 1906) 515–16: "The close of the great struggle of the Church with the empire and the end of the Crusades henceforward narrowed the horizon of the Papacy. One stone after another fell from its gigantic structure; the world withdrew its allegiance, and the sceptre of Innocent III began to drop from the wearied hands of the popes."

of the Joachimites and the Ghibellines, the declining relations between *Imperium* and *Sacerdotium*. Viewed against
this foreboding background, the conclave which assembled
at Perugia in the Spring of 1292 was to be of the utmost
importance to the Church. The election of the new pope
devolved on twelve cardinals—six Romans, four Italians and
two Frenchmen—who in accord with the spirit of the time
were bitterly divided in their loyalty to the Colonna or Ori-
sini families and their sympathy for the Guelph or Ghibel-
line factions. While these two highly self-centered groups
who constituted the college of cardinals bargained and
wrangled over the election of their candidates, the Chair of
St. Peter remained empty at a period which should have
proved decisive for the maintenance of its traditional supremacy and moral prestige in Christendom. On July 5,
1294, two years and three months after the death of Nicholas IV, Pietro di Murrone, monk, hermit and ascetic was
elected Celestine V.[2] His choice was born of hopelessness,
frustration and compromise.

The election of Celestine V exemplifies the disaster to
which incompetence, egoism and bad will can bring the
Church. It also exemplifies the fact, too often overlooked,
that the successor of St. Peter, if he be a saint, must also be
an intelligent, prudent, skilled administrator thoroughly acquainted with the internal and external problems of the
Church over which he presides. Before his election to the
papacy in his seventy-ninth year, Pietro di Murrone had

[2] Celestine V (St. Peter di Murrone), founder of the Celestine
Order, is the only pope, who reigned between Gregory VII (d. 1085)
and Pius V (d. 1572), to be canonized.

spent almost sixty-eight years of his life as a simple monk.
In fact, grown restless with organized religious life, he had
forsaken his monastery to become a recluse in the solitary
wilderness of Mt. Majella where he lead a mortified existence in imitation of the harsh asceticism of his model, St.
John the Baptist. A contemporary biographer tells us "that
he was not endowed with much knowledge because God had
elected the stupid of this world to confound the strong";[3]
and the bull of canonization describes him as "a man of
wondrous simplicity, and unskilled in those matters which
touch on the administration of the universal Church."[4]
This simple, unlettered, unskilled man succeeded in the
course of his short pontificate in creating that climate in
which the disaster of the subsequent two centuries was
born. He is the first, though guiltless, member of a long
chain of errors that make up the historical events of the so
called pre-Reformation papacy.

Celestine V was pope from July 5 to December 13, 1294
—five months in which the papacy was under the thumb of
the French King of Naples, Charles II. In the midst of the
many crucial questions touching on both Church and State
which demanded the attention of a skilled administrator,
Celestine devoted his energies more and more to his personal asceticism which at times bordered on the bizarre.[5]
The simplicity, naïveté and inexperience, which character-

---

[3] *Vita et Miracula Sancti Petri Caelestini* 9, edit. *Analecta Bol-
landiana* 9 (1890) 153.
[4] Cf. the bull of canonization of Clement V, *Qui Facit Magna*
(May 5, 1313). His feast day is May 19th.
[5] For example, he constructed in the Castel Nuovo (Naples) a
little hut in which he lived as a hermit.

ize his short pontificate, made him prey to the unscrupulous, created administrative problems which plagued his successors, and ultimately opened the way to the Avignon papacy. But the best proof of the good will of this old saint, now in his eightieth year, was his willingness to resign the papacy in view of the calamity which he saw issuing from his general ineptitude. On December 13th, after publishing a bull on the right of the pope to resign his office,[6] he surrendered the papal insignia into the hands of the cardinals, descended the pontifical throne and humbly seated himself on the floor. This brave act was greeted with universal sorrow, for the venerable pope had been recognized as a saint even in his life. The humility which inspired his abdication is rare in the history of the Church. Without ever having set foot in Rome as pope, he 'retired' to the castle of Fumone, where he died on May 19, 1296.[7]

The short reign of pope Celestine V is both instructive and prophetic. Compared with the pontificate of Innocent III (d. 1216), who was elected almost one century before the death of Celestine, it shows that downward direction in which the papacy was slowly but surely moving. The sharp contrast between the position of the Holy See at the opening and closing of the thirteenth century is striking. Where-

[6] The formula of renunciation was signed Dec. 13, 1294: "I, Celestine V, motivated by legitimate reasons . . . freely resign the papacy and expressly renounce its station and dignity, burden and honor. From this moment I yield to the sacred college of cardinals the full and free authority of electing and canonically providing a pope for the universal Church."

[7] The harsh, even cruel imprisonment to which Celestine in retirement is said to have been submitted by order of Boniface VIII, has never been conclusively proved. But he held the former pope under 'house-arrest' until his death.

as Innocent III had mastered the Empire, Celestine was enslaved by the House of Valois. The movement is from exaltation to moderation, to depression foreboding domination or absorption by the State. For in this century the new Statism, inspired by the renaissance of Roman law and embodied in the person of Philip the Fair (d. 1314), clearly emerges as the powerful antagonist of the Holy See which it was to torment century after century creating crisis after crisis in all spheres of her activity.

Before the year 1294 had ended, Cardinal Benedict Gaetani, a skilled canon lawyer, a man of considerable experience in the business of the Curia, the very antithesis of his saintly, incompetent predecessor, was elected pope (December 24, 1294) and took the name Boniface VIII. The turbulent pontificate of this pope, so vilified throughout the centuries by his enemies of which there was and has been no lack,[8] forms a clear dividing line between one phase of papal history and another. "The nine-years reign of Boniface VIII," writes Philip Hughes,[9] "was to be one of the most momentous in all Church History; it is, indeed, generally regarded as marking the end of an epoch, and the beginning of the new age when the popes and religion gradually cease to be taken into account as factors in the public life of the Christian nations." Clearly the time demanded "a saint who was also a political genius; it was given no more

[8] Dante places Boniface, who did not fear "to seize the comely Lady [the Church] by deceit, and then to make havoc of her," in the third chasm of hell. Cf. Inferno, Canto XIX, 46–60. Even as late as 1518 Luther raged against "the outrageous tyranny of Boniface VIII, who, as the proverb declares, 'came in as a wolf, reigned as a lion, and died as a dog.'" Cf. R. Bainton, Here I Stand (New York 1951), p. 90.

[9] P. Hughes, A History of the Church 3 (London 1947) 57, 58.

than an extremely competent, experienced official" . . . a man whose public life was tainted with nepotism and who was generally not open to criticism.[10]

It is a paradox of Church History that this pope, who resumed in himself the medieval heritage of papal suprem- acy, unwittingly assisted at the dissolution of all the efforts of the papacy in this direction since the days of Gregory VII (d. 1085). The climate, both political and religious, of the late thirteenth century needed a pope of deep insight, finesse of judgment, breadth of vision, above all a pope with a keen sense of growth and development. History has shown that Boniface by character and disposition was not equipped to handle the great problems of his day. His mind, perfectly in tune with the thought of an earlier phase of history, devised solutions that were out of harmony with the times. Thus his brusque intervention in world-affairs was unwelcomed and unsuccessful. It was not encumbent on Boniface to master history, but rather courageously, boldly and realistically, to face the crisis which it presented; and, if possible, to control and manage it within the re- sources at his disposal; at all events, not to precipitate the unforgettable storm which he brought down on Christen- dom.

If Boniface was unable to understand the significance of the central issues of his day, neither was he able to under-

[10] One of the charges brought against him was that 'he did not seek counsel from the cardinals to follow it, but rather exacted con- sent from them for whatsoever he himself wished.' Note his rude remark to Joannes Monachus: 'Pig-head from Picardy, I want no advice from asses like you.' Cf. B. Tierney, *Foundations of the Con- ciliar Theory* (Cambridge 1955), pp. 181–82.

stand the most formidable adversaries of his policy. The
contest in which he engaged the throne of France in the
person of Philip the Fair (ever so more violent than the
German emperors in their historic struggle with the popes)
was to prove his undoing, but even more than that, it was
to pull down the whole grand edifice which the medieval
papacy had so carefully erected. This French king was a
tireless worker on behalf of his beloved *Gallia*, a realist, a
pragmatist, a courageous fighter, a fearless opponent, a politician of a thousand different tricks, and an invariable win-
ner. He was not a man of many ideas, but those which he
had were meaningful to him; and the goals, which he envisioned, were always attainable. Philip abounded in resources, and was surrounded by a similar brood of crafty and
unscrupulous co-workers whose every plan devised for him
was marked with efficiency and practicality. The whole
habit of mind and way of life of the young French king represented the new national State, a reality with which Boniface, the medieval man and the student of canonical texts,
seemed to have no deep acquaintance. Philip not only dif-
fered with Boniface on issues of state but more than that,
he hated him personally unto death and long afterwards.
Unfortunately history confronted them on opposite sides of
a burning issue—papal supremacy over Christendom.

On February 25, 1296 Boniface issued his famed bull,
Clericis laicos infestos, which was aimed at "the horrible
abuses of the secular power" in France, where the royal government was demanding that clergy as well as laity pay their
share of taxes. This new fiscal arrangement was part of the
vast reorganization to which Philip the Fair was submitting

his kingdom in view of the important international role for which it was being shaped. In the eyes of Boniface taxation of the clergy represented an infringement on their privileged status in the realm, but even more than that it exemplified the traditional hostility of the laity to the clergy. Thus he writes:[11]

Boniface, Bishop, Servant of the servants of God, in perpetual memory of this matter. Antiquity shows us that the laity has always been exceeding hostile to the clergy; and this the experience of the present time clearly demonstrates, since, not content with their limitations, the laity strive for forbidden things and give free reign to the pursuit of illicit gain.

This preamble, hardly to be matched for its tactlessness, not only gave official recognition to anti-clericalism, but in offending the laity, it gave new life to that poisonous laicism which is so hostile to the hierarchic Church.[12] In attempting to subtract the clergy of France from the royal power, Boniface was sustaining a thesis on papal supremacy that had been successfully negated a century before by Henry II in his contest with St. Thomas Becket.[13] And at the same

[11] C. J. Barry (ed.), Readings in Church History 1 (Westminster 1960) 464.

[12] In this connection a remark of J. Lortz, Die Reformation in Deutschland 1 (Freiburg 1949) 10, is noteworthy: "The Reformation is a revolutionary uprising against the papal Church by a theological lay movement. Everything which fostered the hostility of the laity for the papacy and the Church belongs among the causes of the Reformation."

[13] In his struggle with the king, Thomas "was face to face with pain, imprisonment, perhaps even death, and that, not for a principle but in a feudal, personal, quarrel; he would pass into oblivion and pope and king would pick up the threads of their old life while he lay in prison or in the grave." Cf. D. Knowles, "Archbishop Thomas Becket," The Raleigh Lecture on History, Proceedings of the British Academy 35 (1949) 13.

time in his preoccupation with this peripheral question he lost sight of the central issue—the essential relationship of the Holy See to this new and powerful national monarchy.

Face to face with the mighty French kingdom in the person of Philip the Fair and his notorious entourage—William Nogaret, Robert of Artois, Pierre Flote, the Count of St. Pol and the others—Boniface found himself surrounded by representatives of the strong, ruthless modern State which realistically decides issues on the basis of power. "We hold both the swords," Boniface is reported as saying to the royal agent, and Flote as replying, "Truly, Holy Father, but, your swords are but a phrase, and ours a reality."[14] Granted the secular, even irreligious, aims and purposes of this powerful young king, Boniface could only see in him a monarch who would either master the papacy, or lead the Church of France into irreparable schism. Under no circumstances would this highly self-centered monarch assume that traditional role which history had once assigned to *Imperium*.

It is not really surprising that Boniface, aware of the historic contest between Gregory VII and Henry IV, looked to the past to find the weapons which would prove most decisive in his present defense of the honor of the Holy See. On December 5, 1301, he addressed to Philip the bull *Ausculta Fili* with salutary warnings on the obligations of the king to the pope, the divinely constituted shepherd of the flock of Christ. Boniface's teaching here was traditional to the core. His claims were historical and canonical. Even in the royal answer to the papal bull we can

[14] Cf. P. Hughes, *op. cit.*, 3, 76.

hear the defiant echoes of past history.[15] On April 10, 1302 the representatives of the clergy and laity of France, assembled in Notre Dame of Paris, were called upon by Flote to support their king against the outrageous demands of Boniface, "heretic . . . antichrist . . . who at the moment occupies the seat of government in the Church." Significantly, but not surprisingly, the response of the laity was unanimously affirmative.

When the proceedings of the assembly in Notre Dame finally became known to Boniface, he flatly denounced Flote, Robert of Artois and the Count of Pol as the chief instigators of this unwarranted attack on the Holy See, prophesied their evil demise,[16] and summoned the French clergy into a council at Rome to examine the whole question of the state of religion in France.[17] From this assembly, which was held in November 1302, came the celebrated bull *Unam Sanctam* (Nov. 18, 1302) which, as the last pronouncement of the medieval papacy, resumes its perennial claim to supremacy over all power in this world:[18]

[15] Cf. the letter of Henry IV to Gregory VII, January 24, 1076: "Henry, king, not through usurpation but through the holy ordination of God, to Hildebrand, at present not pope but false monk. . . . Descend! Descend, to be damned throughout the ages!" Cf. C. Barry, *op. cit.*, 1. 244–45. This same violent spirit animated the reply of Philip IV to Boniface.

[16] Within a matter of months, at the battle of the Golden Spurs, on July 11, 1302, all three whom Boniface had denounced by name were dead.

[17] It is on this occasion that Boniface is supposed to have made the astonishing remark: "Thrice have our predecessors deposed a king of France . . . though we are not worth our predecessors' feet . . . we would throw out this king as though he were a footman. . . ."

[18] Cf. S. Ehler and J. Morrall, *Church and State through the Centuries* (London 1954), pp. 90–2.

That there is only one Holy, Catholic and Apostolic Church we are compelled to believe and to hold, our faith urging us, and this we do firmly believe and simply confess; and also that there is no salvation or remission of sins outside of her. . . . We are taught by the words of the Gospel that in this Church and in its power there are two swords, a spiritual, to wit, and a temporal. . . . Both are in the power of the Church . . . the one, indeed, to be wielded for the Church, the other by the Church; the former by the priest, the latter by the hands of kings and knights, but at the will and sufferance of the priest. For it is necessary that one sword should be under another, and that the temporal authority should be subjected to the spiritual. . . . We declare, state, define and pronounce that it is altogether necessary to salvation for every human creature to be subject to the Roman Pontiff.

Boniface presented "the supremacy of the apostolic see according to the established formula which he believed to be immutable. Untouched by hesitation, disdaining to ease the shock, he thrust it boldly upon an age already in revolt; there was no wish here to suit the mood of the times nor even any effort at adaptation."[19] He was convinced of the justice of his cause and he was ready to maintain it against all contradictors.[20]

The French court answered the challenge of *Unam Sanctam* in its own brutal way: by vilification, slander, denunciation; by appeal to a general council over the pope; and finally by the disgraceful, shocking attack on the pope's per-

[19] J. Rivière, *Le Problème de l'Église et de l'état* (Louvain 1926), p. 94.

[20] The psychology, underlying Boniface's thought, is well delineated in his discourse of April 30, 1303: "And we boldly declare that, if all the princes on earth were today gathered together against us and against the Church, so long as we possess truth and stand for truth, we would not consider them worth a straw. And surely we would indeed fear, if we did not possess truth and justice. For otherwise we would confuse all and the truth would confuse them." *Ibid.*, p. 94, n. 3.

son at Anagni, September 7, 1303, one of the most dramatic episodes in the whole history of the medieval Church.[21] Humiliated, broken in spirit, reviled and hounded by the king's agents, Boniface died in Rome some weeks later, on October 11th.

The death of Boniface, however, did not terminate the bitter struggle between Philip and the Holy See. The royal hatred, which had persecuted the pope in his lifetime, now furiously followed him after death. Though his successor Bl. Benedict XI, confidant and loyal supporter of Boniface as pope, and faithful to him to the end, mitigated the provisions of the bull *Clericis laicos* and made an honorable peace with the French court, he had the courage to condemn and excommunicate both William of Nogaret and Sciarra Colonna, for their outrageous treatment of Boniface at Anagni. Condemned, they were ordered to appear before the pope by the feast of St. Peter, June 29, 1304, to render account for their criminal actions. Contumaciously they refused; but before a formal process could be opened against them, the pope was dead, very suddenly and very mysteriously, at Perugia, on July 7, 1304.

Almost one year later (June 5, 1305) a Frenchman, Bertrand de Got, of Bordeaux, was elected pope. Five months later, in November, he was crowned at Lyons in the presence of his old friend Philip whose kingdom he never deserted throughout his pontificate. With this French pope, who took the name Clement V, a new phase of papal

[21] Though Boniface had planned to excommunicate Philip, the bull, *Super Petri Solio*, dated Sept. 8, 1303, was never formally promulgated.

history, the Avignon papacy, begins. In many respects
Clement V was well qualified for the high office to which
he had been elected. His knowledge of canon law was expert, he was thoroughly skilled in the machinery of administration, and he had more than ordinary experience in
papal diplomacy. But as a victim to poor health which
reduced considerably his physical and mental strength, he
lacked the energy to fight off the unjust demands of the
royal house of France, to resist its overwhelming attack
on papal independence, to stem the absorption of the papacy
into the orbit of the kingdom of France. And then, too,
there hung over the head of Clement the king's constant
demand that Boniface and his pontificate be solemly condemned by the pope.

Separated from Rome and the loyal supporters of the
Holy See, Clement yielded little by little. He was no match
for the massive political forces working against him. Point
by point he yielded to the French crown. On February 1,
1306 he conditionally withdrew the bulls *Unam Sanctam*
and *Clericis laicos*; and under pressure to condemn Pope
Boniface, in wild desperation, almost under compulsion, he
supported that shameful legal assault on the Knights Tem-
plar which ultimately resulted in their extinction. In involv-
ing the papacy in this sordid manoeuver, a scheme from
which Philip hoped to profit financially, the honor of the
Holy See as a seat of justice was badly damaged.[22] That an
ecumenical council, convoked at Vienne in 1311–12, con-
curred in this conspiracy against the unfortunate Knights

[22] Cf. the highly interesting note in P. Hughes, *op. cit.*, 3. 96, n.
1.

does not in the slightest mitigate the blame which Clement merited.[23]

In the history of the Church Clement V is known as the pope who definitively established the papacy at Avignon. His successor, the astute John XXII (1316–34), and all the popes for the following seventy years until the time of Gregory XI (d. 1378 at Rome) remained there in exile, far from the Eternal City. This unfortunate chapter of papal history, known as the Babylonian Captivity,[24] is characterized by the deep shadows of nationalism which fall across it. For it was a French papacy in the kingdom of France under the protection of the French King. It is precisely this irresponsible commitment of the Avignon papacy which is most censurable. For in removing itself from Rome, the traditional seat and center of the Church, it entered the dark ways of particularism, a fertile source of discontent and reproach to the nations of Christendom. The national atmosphere, which surrounded the Avignon papacy, harmed its moral prestige in the eyes of men who were accustomed to regard Rome as the seat of the universal Church.

[23] The words of Clement V's bull, Vox in excelso dated March 22, 1312, are worth careful consideration: "Then, our most dear son in Christ, Philip, illustrious king of the French, to whom the crimes of [the Templars] had been reported, not through greed—for it was his intention neither to claim nor to appropriate any of the property of the Templars, indeed in his own kingdom he renounced it by totally withdrawing his hand from it—but out of love of the orthodox faith . . . sent us much important information through his legates and through his letters." Cf. Conciliorum oecumenicorum decreta (Freiburg 1962), p. 313.

[24] This opprobrious title emerged from the circle of the humanists (e.g., Petrarch) who gathered like flies at the Court of Avignon.

The seven Avignon popes as a group were neither corrupt, decadent, ineffectual nor disinterested. The greater majority of them were good men, capable administrators, competent in the canon law, and devoted to their work. In their zeal for good government they sinned by excess in that they allowed the Church to move more and more in the direction of centralization, both in administration and in finance. The closely knit system of government and taxation, which resulted from the Avignon centralization, paved the way for the grave discontent and exploitation which characterize the following century and which form the nucleus around which abuses of every sort were to clutter. But even more dangerous than the legal system itself was the large number of petty officials who followed the papal court to Avignon to make their fortune. The secular atmosphere, which these hangers-on engendered, became a scandal and a reproach to the papacy.[25]

One of the surest tests of the vigor and health of Catholic intellectual life is the quality of her theological thinking. The one hundred years after the death of St. Thomas Aquinas (d. 1274), the *Doctor Communis*, show unmistakable signs of deterioration. The persistent drift is away from his school of thought with its firm trust in metaphysics, its deep appreciation of speculation and its confident reliance on the power of the human mind as an instrument of

[25] Petrarch, for example, characterized Avignon as "the wicked Babylon, the hell of the living, the sink of iniquity. There," he continues, "one finds neither faith nor charity nor religion nor fear of God nor shame, no truth, nothing holy. . . . Of all the cities, which I know, it is the most stinking. . . ." Cf. G. Mollat, *Les papes d'Avignon* (Paris 1949), p. 441.

truth. "It was the unfortunate effect of the great thinkers who followed St. Thomas that their theories of knowledge destroyed the all important nexus between the spheres of reason and faith, when they denied the power of reason really to prove the existence of God."[26] The tragedy of fourteenth century theology is to be sought in the sharp cleavage which it placed between faith and reason—a cleavage which ultimately forced the Christian thinker to seek security in an arbitrary voluntarism of one hue or another.

The most striking example of deterioration of Catholic thought in this century is in the area of political science. The appearance in June 24, 1324 of the *Defensor Pacis* of Marsilius of Padua, one time Rector of the University of Paris, marks a veritable stage in the development of theories of Church–State relations.[27] This revolutionary work—filled with scorn and contempt for the Church—emerged from the anti-papal circle of Ludwig the Bavarian, William Ockham, Jean de Jadun, the Franciscan Spirituals and the other malcontents of that day. It was the most direct and pernicious assult launched up to that time against the supremacy of the spiritual in this world, for it proposed to remake Christendom by situating the Church within the State as a phase of her civil life, to negate the distinction between clergy and laity, to hand over the ecclesiastical *magisterium* to the civil administration, and to reduce

[26] Cf. P. Hughes, *op. cit.*, 3, 115.

[27] Cf. A. Gewirth, *Marsilius of Padua, the Defender of Peace*, 2 Vols. (New York 1951), 56. This is a very useful introduction to, commentary on, and translation of the *Defensor Pacis*.

the ministry of the Church to a public service. The whole import of the *Defensor Pacis* was to force the Church into the sacristy far away from public life, to allot her no more than a passive role in world affairs, and to annihilate her as an independent religious institution.

The errors of Marsilius were indeed condemned by John XXII in *Licet iuxta doctrinam* of October 28, 1327;[28] but surprisingly no Catholic theoretician stepped forward to refute the heresiarch on the merits of the question itself. Translated into French, Italian and German, the *Defensor* became in a short time the vademecum of the Hussites, the Gallicans, the Conciliarists and all those who were united in their opposition to the papacy. It was a book the extent of whose evil influence is too vast to be measured. Yet in reading the history of this time one searches in vain for the formation of a program or plan of study and research which might have stemmed or at least controlled the flow of this seditious thought. Latent in the *Defensor* is the conviction, perhaps not fully realized by even Marsilius himself, that the Church as an external institution existing side by side with the State was in need of reform to bring it up to date with new developments which were taking place in the world of politics. The alert theologians of this period should have been ready to sift the thought of Marsilius more carefully, to examine his new viewpoint more closely. In the clash of ideas new patterns might have been discovered along which the Church could have developed its

[28] The condemned propositions are printed in *Enchiridion Symbolorum*, ed. A. Schönmetzer, S.J. (32nd ed. Freiburg 1963), pp. 289–90.

own constitution. Without being a reformer, Marsilius might have stimulated reform. His mentality was far too fanatical to have been of positive service to the Church; but his *Defensor*, if properly assessed, might have offered valuable insight into the future. It is clear to us now that the significance of his work escaped the generality of theologians. The solemn condemnation did not solve the difficult problems which it raised, and his theories returned again and again to plague the papacy.

Throughout the fourteenth and fifteenth centuries deterioration weakened two other important aspects of Catholic life—worship and *ascetica*. The liturgy, following a pattern which had formed in the early Middle Ages, withdrew more and more from reality. Accessories continued to accumulate, and this accumulation tended to obscure the true mystery of both Word and Sacrament. Devotions to the saints grew out of proportion to their value and even tended to supplant, at least in the popular mind, Christ as the one true Mediator. Processions multiplied. The quantity and quality of relics were exaggerated. The Gospel yielded more and more to legend; and popular preaching, far from being concerned with theology, was largely devoted to morality. The Christ of prayer was invariably the historical Christ, the Christ of 'then,' rather than the Glorious Christ, the Christ of 'now.' The external aspect of the Church, the hierarchy, came more and more into full light, while the internal aspect of the Church, the Mystical Body, receded into shadow. The division of priest and laity into two distinct classes became acute. Reception of the Eucharist as sacramental *food* decreased sharply as ever greater stress was placed on the Eucharist as sacramental presence. The celebration of the Mass, now withdrawn far back into the dark Gothic apse, became a 'mysterious' rite which the faithful witnessed from the nave rather than shared. The whole tragic picture of divine worship in the autumn time of the Middle Ages is only presented here because as one of the essential ingredients of the general decadence of the times, it will offer ammunition to the reformers of the sixteenth century.[29]

The spiritual life of the late fourteenth century also shows symptoms of decay. To a great extent expressed in the so called *Devotio Moderna*, this spirituality was largely formed under the influence of the Brethren of the Common Life and the Windesheim Canons; and from the circle of Gerard de Groote (d. 1384) at Deventer, it had spread rapidly throughout Europe with far reaching success. This new spirituality, so simple, direct, personal and almost non-sectarian, essentially aimed at a homely piety, untouched by learning. It was in many respects a direct reaction to the speculative, metaphysical, learned spirituality of the German mystics and their mystical doctrine. The *Devotio* invited the Christian to concentrate on the love of God, to seek interior peace through acceptance of God's Will and to acquire solid virtue as the fruit of systematic meditation and pious reading. But latent within the movement was a sharp divorce between theology and piety which

[29] A good, general treatment of the historical development of the liturgy from antiquity to the Late Middle Ages is presented by J. Jungmann, "The Defeat of Teutonic Arianism and the Revolution in Religious Culture in the Early Middle Ages," in *Pastoral Liturgy* (New York 1962), pp. 1–101.

was every bit as real and dangerous as the cleavage between
faith and reason. In depressing the role which both theology and metaphysics must play in the formation of
spiritual doctrine, it opened the door to that pernicious
voluntarism whose full import would become manifest only
much later.[30]

Thus one hundred and fifty years after the death of Innocent III (d. 1216), who had brought the Church to a
high water-mark of achievement, Christendom was in serious trouble. The papacy had forsaken universal Rome for
provincial Avignon. Overwhelmed by the power of the
royal house of France, it freely entered the circle of French
influence. In the person of Innocent VI (1352–62) it sat
by in silence, as Charles IV in the Golden Bull of January
13, 1356 virtually dissolved the old Sacerdotium-Imperium
alliance. Theology, the venerable 'queen of the sciences,'
tended more and more to relinquish her role as biblical ex-
egete in favor of the new dialectica. And this overbalanced
commitment to dialectica distracted her increasingly from
the current problems which beset Christianity. Faith and
reason, piety and theology, clergy and laity moved further
and further apart. Within the university, once cultivated
and nourished by the papacy, the seed of anti-papalism
began to grow. Administration and finance absorbed the
attention of the popes, while the quality of the episcopacy
gradually sank and the spiritual formation of the clergy
suffered. New national monarchies, which freely repudiated
the claims of Unam Sanctam and all that it represented, occupied the center of the stage, and brought with them a

[30] Cf. J. Leclercq, La spiritualité du Moyen Age (Paris 1961), pp.
512–25.

pronounced secularism which especially manifested itself
in anti-clericalism and anti-papalism. Christendom was indeed in serious trouble.

Throughout the seventy years which the popes spent in
Avignon there were serious-minded Catholics who dis-
tinctly recalled that the true seat of the papacy was Rome
and who sharply protested its voluntary exile so detrimental
to the universal good of the Church. One of them was St.
Bridget of Sweden (d. 1373), another was St. Catherine
of Siena (d. 1380)—two of the most remarkable women
of their century. The sharp words which they directed to
the Avignon popes are worth recalling here in view of the
fact that these women, more than anyone else in Christendom, fearlessly raised their voices on behalf of the Church
of Rome, which they loved so dearly. Their writings are
among the treasures of Christian literature, and their holy
lives attest that God never leaves His Church without
saints.

When the French pope Urban V (1362–70) after a brief
visit to Rome in 1367–70—a feeble attempt to restore the
papacy there—resolved to return to Avignon, St. Bridget
addressed these word to him that came to her, as she said,
"as though from a radiant sun":[31]

I am the Mother of God . . . I will speak to you of the pope
who is named Urbanus. To him the Holy Spirit gave the counsel
that he should come to Rome to work justice and strengthen the
Christian faith and renew the Holy Church . . . I led him to
Rome by my prayers. But what does he do now? Now he turns
his back on me and not his face and would leave me. And a false
and evil spirit would entice him to do this. For it wearies him to
do his duty, and he is longing for ease and comfort. He is long-

[31] J. Jörgensen, *Saint Bridget of Sweden* 2 (London 1954) 221.

ing for his own country, and his carnally minded friends urge him to depart, for they think more of his temporal welfare and conform more to his will than to the will of God and to what serves the glory of God and the everlasting good of the Pope. . . . If he should succeed in getting back to his own country he will be struck such a blow that his teeth will shake in his mouth. His sight will be darkened and all his limbs will tremble. . . . The friends of God will no longer include him in their prayers, and he will be called to account to God for what he did and what he did not.

On September 16, 1370 Urban V returned to France. Within three months he was dead and buried, according to Petrarch, "among the great sinners in Avignon."[32]

Within a matter of days (December 29, 1370) Gregory XI, the restorer of the papacy to Rome, was elected at Avignon. Before long he had the following letter from St. Catherine:[33]

. . . This is what I wish to see in you. And if up to this time, we have not stood very firm, I wish and pray in truth that the moment of time which remains be dealt with manfully, following Christ, whose vicar you are, like a strong man. And fear not, Father, for anything that may result from those tempestuous winds that are now beating against you, those decaying members which have rebelled against you. Fear not! For divine aid is near. Have a care for spiritual things alone, for good shepherds, good rulers, in your cities. . . . Give us, then, a remedy; and comfort you in Christ Jesus, and fear not. . . . Up, then, Father, and no more negligence! Raise the gonfalon of the most holy Cross, for with the fragrance of the Cross you shall win peace. . . . Comfort you! Comfort you! And come! Come to console the poor,

[32] *Ibid.*, p. 222. In spite of the prophetic vision of St. Bridget and the mean judgment of Petrarch, Urban is listed among the beatified. His cult was approved by Pius IX in 1870.

[33] V. D. Scudder, *Saint Catherine of Siena* (London 1905), pp. 121–22.

the servants of God, your sons! We await you with eager and loving desire. . . ."

On January 17, 1377 Gregory XI solemnly entered Rome where he remained until his death in the following Spring. The restoration of the papacy to Rome was definitive.

Of the sixteen cardinals, who assembled in Rome on April 7, 1378 to elect a successor to Gregory XI, eleven were French, four Italian and one Spaniard. In the light of the subsequent development of the papacy the results of this conclave were to make it the most stupendous which the Church had witnessed up to that time and since.[34] The cardinal electors, divided into factions (French, Limoges, Italian), were manoeuvering to have that candidate elected who would be most favorable to their national (and personal) interests. Within the conclave there was division, but it was not acute. The pressing danger was from without. The Roman populace, in dread of the election of a French pope and the withdrawal of the papacy to Avignon once again, was clearly of one mind. "Romano lo volemo, o al manco Italiano," it shouted throughout the night of April 7th, and well into the following morning. From all contemporary accounts, the city of Rome was seized by high tension, sparked into general disorder by drunken revelry.[35] There was tumult among the people, violence, shouting,

[34] One of the best treatments of this celebrated conclave and its sequel is W. Ullmann's The Origins of the Great Schism (London 1948).

[35] Ibid., p. 39: "Every witness stresses the disorderly nature of the Roman assembly outside the palace, and even Urban himself referred to the riots of the Romans and offered a plausible explanation; he said that it was "vinolentia" rather than "violentia" which characterized these street scenes outside the palace."

angry threats, and more than once a stormy attempt to in-
vade the very precincts of the palace where the conclave
was being held.

On the morning of April 8, 1378 the conclave announced
that a decision had been finally reached and that Archbishop Bartolomeo Prignano of Bari, now in his sixtieth
year, had been elected Pope Urban VI. He was regarded by
his contemporaries as an experienced, capable Churchman.
For twenty years he had been active at the papal court at
Avignon where he came to know personally the more important people of the day and at Rome his accomplishments
as vice-chancellor proved that he had real administrative
ability. The years which he had spent in both these important centers permitted him to acquire a cosmopolitan
outlook with which the French cardinals were sufficiently
impressed. He was generally known to be a simple man—
peaceful, devout, and friendly. The Italians were satisfied
with his election. One of their own had been chosen and
the papacy would be fixed at Rome. The cardinals, who had
elected him, openly and freely extended their obedience to
him. The fearful night of April 7–8 seemed to have accomplished much.[36]

But what was unknown to most on the morning of April

36 According to the official, curial document, the *Factum Urbani*,
a kind of white-paper on the conclave, Urban is supposed to have
asked his electors "whether he had been elected sincerely, purely,
freely and canonically by all the cardinals, adding that if the election
had not been carried out canonically and without compulsion he
would not consent to become pope. They answered, firmly and
strongly that the election was performed freely, canonically and
without compulsion." On the truth of this statement the whole
validity of Urban's claim hangs.

8, 1378 was that Urban VI was both a very radical reformer
and a seriously unbalanced tyrant whose uncontrolled, un-
reasonable rages and fury were probably rooted in a mental
sickness. Within days of his election it became apparent that
Urban's determined intention to reform the Church from
the head down would commence with the college of cardinals against whom he directed savage anger, scathing words,
utter contempt, and almost physical violence.[37] In frustration he recklessly claimed power and grandeur on the basis
of which it would be impossible to govern the Church with
prudence and wisdom. The words of Cardinal Robert of
Geneva to Pope Urban are filled with significance: "Unlike
your predecessors, Holy Father, you do not treat the cardinals with that honor which you owe them. You are dimin-
ishing our authority, but verily I tell you that we will do our
best to diminish yours."[38]

Six months later on September 20, 1378, the dissatisfied
college of cardinals, now gathered together at Fondi in the
kingdom of Naples—hence well out of the grasp of Urban
—proceeded to the election of Robert of Geneva who took
the name Clement VII. It was the bold act of a group of
Churchmen who had persuaded themselves that the election of Urban had taken place without freedom. In the
course of the coming months Christendom divided. France
and her allies submitted to Clement, while Germany, Italy,
and England adhered to Urban. "The obedience of Urban
was more numerous, that of Clement more imposing." On

[37] Cf. the interesting incidents related by W. Ullmann, op. cit.,
pp. 44 ff.
[38] Ibid., p. 48.

June 20, 1379, Clement set sail for France to take up resi-
dence at Avignon where he cemented the schism which
divided the Church.[39]

The history of the Great Western Schism is indeed complicated. The initial schism in which the Roman obedience
of Urban VI opposed the Avignon obedience of Clement
VII ultimately grew into a third obedience after the 'con-
ciliatory' Council of Pisa elected Pope Alexander V in 1409.
Thus the unity of the Church and together with it the
unity of the Western World was divided according to their
allegiances to this or that pope. The scandal was enormous.
Even the allegiance of the saints was divided.[40] In the eyes
of the common man the vast moral prestige of the Holy See
was brought down, for obedience to the Chair of St. Peter
was determined for him according to national interest. The
long wrangling and intricate litigations to terminate the
schism fatigued men who began to consider an ecclesiastical
system, which was incapable of securing unity of obedience, to be effete and passé.

At the same time the stubborn impasse to which this
triad of 'papal' powers had brought the Church forced theologians to think out a dangerous new ecclesiology which
sought to establish her on a more secure foundation than
the papacy itself. Here theory followed fact. Because the

[39] The history of the remaining years of the pontificate of Urban
VI (d. 1389) is fabulous. His inhuman treatment of his own cardinals, who had conspired against him, is without parallel in the history of the papacy.
[40] St. Catherine and St. Vincent Ferrer, both Dominicans, divided on this question. The one adhered to Urban and Rome, the
other to Clement and Avignon.

papacy *de facto* was powerless to secure a unified obedience, one concluded that it could not *de jure* be the ultimate principle either of unity or of obedience. Concord and security must be sought elsewhere—in the general council. And now, after seventy years of the Avignon papacy (1308–78), the Great Schism, itself destined to last more than a quarter of a century, created even a greater crisis. It is not surprising, therefore, that the seeds of Conciliarism began at this time to stir with life and to sprout.[41]

Nor is it surprising that at this time John Wycliffe (1329–84), 'the morning star of the Reformation,' appeared on the scene with his *De potestate papae* (ca. 1380) as a bold manifesto of anti-papalism proclaiming to the world the pope as antichrist. Condemned by Gregory XI in 1377, these pernicious errors made their way to far off Bohemia where they captured the furiously patriotic and nationalistic John Hus (1369–1415), the Bohemian rebel. With Hus we find ourselves in the presence of a new development—the heretic and apostate whose message captivates the hearts of a whole nation, rouses it to enthusiastic opposition to Rome on behalf of the beloved Fatherland, creates a strongly anti-papal block in Central Europe which neither excommunication nor crusade can crush. The theology of the *De ecclesia* of Hus foreshadowed the ecclesiology of the reformers of the following century.[42] It is not

[41] Conrad of Gelnhausen's *Epistola Concordiae* (May 1380) is one of the first attempts to express a conciliar theory of the Church.

[42] Cf. E. A. Ryan, "Three Early Treatises on the Church," *Theological Studies* 5 (1944) 113–40, and P. DeVooght, *Hussiana* (Louvain 1960), pp. 9–208.

without reason that Luther would one day be called "the Saxon Hus."

On November 5, 1414, the sixteenth ecumenical council assembled at Constance whither it had been summoned by the Pisan pope John XXIII.[43] Its principal functions were the reform of the Church, the extirpation of heresy, especially that of John Hus, and the restoration of unity in the Church by the acceptance of one universally recognized pope.[44] Because Hus had appealed to an ecumenical council over the authority of the pope, the Fathers of Constance invited him thither to state his case before them. Under the imperial safe-conduct of emperor Sigismund, he appeared in Constance in November 1414. Very shortly after his trial had commenced, he was securely locked away in an ecclesiastical prison. Convicted of contumacious heresy by the council, he was condemned to death and handed over to the secular arm. The tragic history of his last days in prison, filled with love, forgiveness and conviction, almost reads like the acts of an early Christian martyr. Degraded from his sacerdotal office, he was cruelly burnt at the stake on July 6, 1415, in the public square of Constance before the eyes of his accusers. His body was reduced to ashes; but even with that it was allowed no peace, for it was scattered to the wind.[45]

[43] A good summary of the council is given by P. Hughes, The Church in Crisis (New York 1961), pp. 260–73.
[44] The purpose is mentioned in the decree Sacrosancta of April 5, 1415.
[45] The circumstances of the trial, imprisonment, last days and execution of John Hus are treated with detailed clarity by P. De Voogt, L'Hérésie de Jean Huss (Louvain 1960).

It was the end of John Hus's body but not the end of his spirit. It lived on to torment and haunt the Church in a thousand different ways through the centuries; and the problems which he had posed in his life were not solved until many stormy pages of history had been turned. The execution of Hus only demonstrated that difficulties of the spirit can never be solved by the sword; that problems, which are buried alive in one century, only rise once again in another; and, that while history falls under the judgment of God, it also falls under the judgment of man.

In the twelfth session of the council on May 29, 1415, John XXIII was deposed for his surreptitious flight, for his simony, and for his bad life. He was forthwith led away to a prison in Germany.[46] On July 4, 1415 Gregory XII resigned his claim to the papacy and retired in peace. But the Spaniard Benedict XIII (Pedro de Luna) ignored the council, stubbornly retained his papal title, and continued to live on for years as pope, secluded in the solitary splendor of his Spanish castle. In spite of his uncooperative spirit, the Council, now that the Great Schism had been terminated, proceeded to the problem of securing the unity of the Church.

[46] Set free in 1419, he was made Cardinal Bishop of Tusculum by Martin V whom he recognized. He was buried in the Baptistery at Florence. His tomb (by Donatello and Michelozzo) is enscribed: 'Ioannes quondam papa XXIII . . .'

III

Councils of Constance and Basle

The ecclesiastical sources of the first part of the fifteenth century are almost unanimous in the witness they bear to the universal demand for a thorough reform of the Church. "The whole world," writes a contemporary theologian, "the clergy, all Christian people, know that a reform of the Church militant is both necessary and expedient. Heaven and the elements demand it. It is called for by the Sacrifice of the Precious Blood mounting up to heaven. The very stones will soon be constrained to join in the cry."[1] The fathers of the Council of Constance, fully aware that ecclesiastical reform was one of the paramount needs of the hour, struggled with the problem, contrived various ways and means, wandered lost in a maze of subsidiary detail. Their aspirations were clear, their measures halfhearted, and their accomplishment insignificant.[2]

[1] L. Pastor, *The History of the Popes* 1 (London 1891) 202–203.
[2] The disappointment was great. High hopes had been pinned on the Council. Thus John XXIII in an Apostolic Brief of October 31, 1413 had written: ". . . the ancient Fathers held frequent general councils to maintain concord and unity in the Church. But later, in modern times, for many years councils have been omitted and neglected to the terrible jeopardy of the whole Church. Since that

The contrivance of a reform program at Constance was further complicated and jeopardized by the multiple factions into which the members of the Council were divided. The four Nations, Germany, England, France, and Italy—to which Spain was later added—were split, and, in a sense, rendered powerless, by the particularism of party spirit and national pride. Each Nation envisioned reform from the point of view of its special wants and needs, while the relations between the cardinals and the bishops, between the higher and lower clergy, were seriously disturbed by ill will, mistrust and even hatred.[3] And the fact that the clergy of this period was unable to inspire fellowship and confidence in the laity rendered the situation even more difficult.[4] Nor could unqualified reliance be placed upon the theologians and canonists of the day whose ecclesiology under the influence of Conciliarism deviated widely from the monarchical concept of the Church.

The reform and election decrees which the council finally

<hr>

omission how many calamities have befallen us we Catholics all know. . . ." Cf. L. R. Loomis, *The Council of Constance* (New York 1961), p. 72.

[3] The "academic" division of the Council into Nations, "framed with the sole purpose of counteracting the preponderance of the Italian prelates," resulted in the failure of systematic reform. At the Council the bold proposal was made to exclude the Cardinals from its discussions on both union and reform. Cf. L. Pastor, *op. cit.*, 1, 203.

[4] Cf. J. Huizinga, *The Waning of the Middle Ages* (New York 1924), p. 178: "Of all the contradictions which religious life of the period presents, perhaps the most insoluble is that of an avowed contempt of the clergy, a contempt seen as an undercurrent throughout the Middle Ages, side by side with the very great respect shown for the sanctity of the sacerdotal office." Cf. also L. Pastor, *op. cit.*, 1, 203.

published in its fortieth General Session on October 30, 1417 envisioned reformation as a task to be undertaken by the pope after his election.[5] Both the Nations and the Cardinals had agreed that the pope, once elected, was "to take measures for ecclesiastical reform, especially in reference to the Supreme Head of the Church and the Roman Court."[6] It was a straight, simple request for a general reformation touching all members of the Church, but especially the administration of the Roman Curia. And the new pope, now that the Great Schism was resolved, was to meet with the Nations or their representatives before the dissolution of the council in order to work out a concrete, realistic plan for the renovation of the whole Church.

One month later, on St. Martin's Day, November 11, 1417, Cardinal Oddo Colonna was unanimously elected pope in the Merchants' Hall at Constance. With the coming of Martin V to the papal throne the scandalous schismatic breach in the papacy was de jure healed, for he was recognized by practically the totality of Western Christendom as the one, true, sovereign Pope;[7] and, in virtue of the reform decree of the fortieth General Session he had a conciliar mandate to look to the reform and renewal of the Church, especially the thorough restoration of the Holy See ravaged by the forty dread years (1378–1417) of schism. The task which history assigned this inadequate pope—

[5] This compromise, proposed by Henry Beaufort, Bishop of Winchester, opened the stuborn impasse to which the Council had come in the matter of the relation of the papacy to reform.

[6] Cf. L. Pastor, op. cit., 1, 207.

[7] Though the anti-pope Clement VIII (Aegius Muñoz, a cardinal once attached to the Curia of Benedict XIII) only submitted to Martin V in 1429, no one of importance took him, or Benedict XIII, who lived on in Spain until 1423, seriously.

almost one century to the day before the publication of Luther's theses—was by all standards enormous, far beyond his personal capacity and energy. For through him one hoped for a general renewal of the Church, that general reformation which Paul III (1534–49) initiated only at a later date, in the Tridentine age (1545–63).

In answer to the Council's decree of October 30th requesting a thorough renovation of the Church, Martin submitted on January 20, 1418 a draft of eighteen reforms mainly based on the different suggestions which had been made by the Nations.[8] On March 21st, in the forty-third General Session of the Council, seven general decrees, in distinction to the particular decrees drawn up to meet the needs of each Nation, were promulgated for the reform of the entire Church. They were essentially aimed at the regulation and modification of exemptions, benefices, simony, dispensations, tithes, and lastly the manner of life of the clergy. It was especially these decrees which Martin V in virtue of his election to the papacy was to execute for the general reform of the Church.[9]

In reading these seven decrees in the light of subsequent

[8] Among the proposals of the Nations was one aimed at the highly Latin complexion of the College of Cardinals. Martin agreed. "The Cardinals should be chosen proportionally from all parts of Christendom." Then he added the 'saving' phrase, "as much as this shall be possible." And, of course, it was found impossible.

[9] Cf. the evaluation of these decrees in P. Hughes, *A History of the Church* 3, 301–302: "These seven decrees it may be thought are slender fruit indeed after four years of conference between priests and prelates from every part of Christendom, reputedly zealous for the reform of Christian life. . . . Nowhere is there any sign of constructive thinking, and it is surely a notable failure that nowhere is there any care to provide for the formation and better education of the parochial clergy."

history one is struck by the unreal comprehension of the
state of the Church which they reflect in every detail. Their
central preoccupation was administration and finance, for
example, the restriction of privileges, especially papal ex-
emption, the regulation of revenues and tithes, and the
firm control of dispensations. Practically nothing was said
of the reform of Christian piety and morality, nothing of
the sacramental and sacrificial system, the source of grace
and life without which Christian reform is inconceivable.
The clergy in whose hands rests the care of souls were
exhorted, presumably by way of 'reform' to correct their
style (both form and color) of dress, their manner of wearing the hair, and lack of proper decorum at liturgical functions under pain of loss of a month's salary.[10] The cardinals,
a source of special annoyance and scandal at the time, are
to be fixed at twenty-four in number, to be selected on a
more international basis with the membership of the college
limited to churchmen of experience, learning, and quality.[11]

The universal desire and intense longing for reform which
the Fathers of the Council ardently expressed and for which
they had sat in session for four years, miscarried. For the
reform decrees both general and particular were nothing
more than a pretentious ambition never to be fully realized
in the practical order; and even had there been an earnest
attempt to carry out this program, it is questionable
whether real reform would have been achieved. For the
much desired renewal of Christendom demanded something more than the 'legalistic' plans which the Council had

10 *Ibid.*, p. 301.
11 A subsequent chapter of this study will show how poorly the
popes of the fifteenth century observed this reform decree.

formulated and promulgated. It required a radical transformation of all levels of Christian society, an invasion of
the most sensitive aspects of private interest, and an inner
renewal of the spirit of man. In addition to planning and
devising, there was need of courage joined to humility and
action, and an over all direction by competent leadership.
It is a paradox of that exhausted century that the reform
which was most passionately wanted, was also most feared
when it came close to realization.[12]

Encumbered with medieval survivals, victimized by a
privileged class of administrators, prostrate under an effete
bureaucracy, the Church continued throughout the century
to sink even deeper into that morass from which she had
solemnly resolved to extricate herself. This regrettable failure is traceable neither to the bad will of Martin V nor to
the culpable inertia of the Fathers of Constance. The
blame is to be fixed elsewhere—in the dread doctrine of
Conciliarism, the *bête noire* of the fifteenth century papacy.
It colored the ecclesiastical atmosphere of the day with dark
shadows by advancing an ecclesiology, which, if left unchecked, would surely destroy the Church in her essential
constitution. And yet in the concrete order of things Conciliarism and reform were so closely interlocked as to be
almost indistinguishable from one another. In its hard struggle against the evils of the former, the papacy was tragically
forced to neglect the latter.

Theoretically Conciliarism maintained that the Pope and
the bishops of the Church are equally successors of St.
Peter, both heirs to his extensive authority over the Kingdom of God on earth. The Pope, therefore, enjoys a prim-

[12] Cf. L. Pastor, *op. cit.*, 1, 210.

acy of honor, not of authority. As *primus inter pares,* he is
the supreme administrator and custodian of the affairs of
the Church, not her chief judge and legislator endowed
with the special authority of Christ. It is the ecumenical
council as the supreme teaching, judging, and legislating
praesidium, which plays the decisive role; for, deriving its
supremacy from Christ, it represents the total Church, and
is, therefore, constituted above the Pope, who *de jure* it has
the right to control, manage, reform, and, if need be, call to
account and depose. "The Church is a divine cosmos in
which God's will and man's freedom are interlocked." Conciliarism, as a doctrine, demanded that the papacy definitively break with its venerable past by repudiating its claims
to possess uniquely and supremely the heritage of St. Peter.

In the practical order, Conciliarism proceeded from the
conviction that many together can accomplish what one
alone can not. There seems no doubt that the inability or
the unwillingness of the papacy at this time to launch a
gigantic and thorough reform of the Church was an important factor in stimulating the growth of this doctrine
and strengthening its ascendancy in the minds of men. The
disastrous ecclesiastical situation that had dominated Christendom for almost half a century—at first, one pope, then
two, later three, finally two in forced retirement, and one in
disgraceful flight—yields historical insight into the cogency
of the drastic measures prescribed by the Conciliarists.
Their uncontrolled attempt at ecclesiastical reform, born of
fatigue and disgust, represents the last stand of men in the
throes of bewilderment, frustration and anger. At Constance
there were churchmen who never throughout their adult

lives, until the election of Martin V terminated the schism, had known the peace and serenity of a Christendom united under one, sovereign pope, universally recognized and obeyed. If monarchical rule had led the Church into this wilderness, it was the earnest hope of the Conciliarists that the introduction of an aristocratic oligarchy would lead it onward to something better.

The roots of Conciliarism are in evidence far beyond the days of the Council of Constance, perhaps even as early as the canonists of the twelfth century.[13] It was carefully nurtured by both Marsilius of Padua (d. 1342) and William Ockham (d. 1349), and by the commencement of the fifteenth century Conciliarism was in full bloom. The history of its development shows that it was not the child of irresponsible thinkers, though among its devotees can be numbered theologians and canonists whose judgment was not always above question. At Constance both Cardinal Pierre d'Ailly (d. 1420), 'the soul of the council,' and Chancellor John Gerson (d. 1429), doctor Christianissimus and one of the most learned, respected men of that day, favored the revolutionary approach to reformation which Conciliarism imported. In fact, both of these men played a significant role in the preparation of the decree Sacrosancta (April 6, 1415) of Constance, the foundation stone of Gallicanism.[14] Still as far as the sources allow us to judge, both appear to

[13] Cf. H. Jedin, Ecumenical Councils (New York, 1960), pp. 105–8.

[14] For Gallicanism the papacy was the root of all evils. Thus in the days of the Great Schism, Pierre le Roy, the father of Gallicanism, wrote: "The schism will end when obedience is withdrawn from the Pope. . . ."

be churchmen of good will, devoted, sincere, even pious, and intensely interested in the pressing problem of union and of reform. Their novel ecclesiology is typical of the theology of the late medieval scholasticism in which they had been educated.

Apart from his Conciliarism, John Gerson was rightly convinced that the unity and reform of the Church should be rooted in and proceed from the spiritual life of the individual Christian. In the midst of the confusion and obscurity, which the multiple claimants to the papacy had created, he urged prayer, reverence, observance and dignity; and he devoted his best energies to creating an atmosphere of piety and charity, selflessness and generosity in which a peaceful solution of the great schism might be worked out. Central in his thought is the peace of the Church; and, so moving was his quest for this peace that it forced him to subordinate everything to it; even the papacy itself was evaluated only in terms of its ability to pacify Christendom. It is remarkable to note how the subsequent intellectual development of Gerson led him to a sharp reversal of this Conciliarism of his younger years.[15]

The pressing problems, created by the Great Western Schism, could not be ignored, if the Church was to continue her saving mission in this world. The solution was

---

[15] At one time in his career Gerson went so far as to assert that the decree of Constance on the supremacy of the council over the pope should be carved on the portals of every church. His irenic approach to the problems of the Schism is well illustrated by his treatise, On the Unity of the Church (1409). Cf. Advocates of Reform, ed. M. Spinka, Library of the Christian Classics 14 (Philadelphia 1953), 140–48.

admittedly reform in head and members. The crisis was clear, but its resolution depended on the discovery of the proper method and critique; it also was contingent on energy and action. The Conciliarists thrust forth their 'saving' formula—the exaltation of the Council over the pope. The thrust was far too sharp and deep to be accepted without protest from the Curialists. The formula was revolutionary, going beyond the limits of valid reform and ultimately immobilizing the papacy at a decisive moment in history. Reform became associated with Conciliarism, and Conciliarism, because its was incompatible with the monarchical constitution of the Church, was repudiated. And for the Church this was a tragedy whose full significance would only be grasped in the following century, when reform would be sought without benefit of either Church or council.

In the fifth session of the Council of Constance (April 6, 1415), in sheer desperation over the second flight of John XXIII from Constance,[16] a decree was passed on the relation of the papacy to the council which voices the essentials of Conciliarism. It reads:[17]

The sacred synod of Constance, forming a General Council in view of the extirpation of the schism and in view of the union and reformation of God's Church in its head and members . . . first declares that it is lawfully assembled in the Holy Spirit and

[16] The bitterness with which John XXIII's unexpected withdrawal from Constance was greeted is illustrated by the remark of Bishop Vidal of Toulon: "The flight of the pope is a scandal which renders him suspect of connivance with schism and heresy, if he cannot readily justify himself in this matter and make satisfaction for it."

[17] S. Ehler and J. Morrall, Church and State through the Centuries (London 1954), p. 105.

constitutes a General Council, represents the Catholic Church and has immediate power from Christ to which anyone, of whatever status and condition, even if holding the papal dignity, is bound to obey in matters pertaining to the Faith, extirpation of schism and reformation of the said Church in head and members. . . .

It continues by declaring further that anyone, even the pope, who shall disobey the laws, statutes, and ordinations of the council shall be punished and be required to do penance.

The evaluation of this decree, so perfectly mirroring the visage of Conciliarism, poses the delicate ecclesiological questions, whether Constance, as a validly constituted ecumenical synod, gave solemn approval to the doctrine that a council is above the pope; and if it did, whether this decree was accepted by the Holy See; and if it were, how this harmonizes with the decrees of the fourth session (July 18, 1870) of the First Vatican Council. The majority of Catholic theologians answer the first two questions in the negative. Conciliarism received neither ecumenical nor papal approval, for the Church accepted only the last sessions (41–45) of the council as ecumenical, those sessions held after the election of Martin V on November 11, 1417. In this matter the Church's acceptance is decisive. Further, the approval of Martin V was only bestowed on what the earlier sessions of the council had handled "with regard to matters of faith *conciliariter* and in no other fashion or mode."[18] The decree of the Fifth Session, largely the work of the Nations and held without the presence of all the Cardi-

[18] J. Hefele and H. Leclercq, *Histoire des Conciles* 7, 1 (Paris 1916) 211.

nals,[19] was not approved by the pope because it was not handled *conciliariter*. The Fifth Session, therefore, of Constance and the Fourth Session of the Vatican do not clash on a dogmatic level.

Recently this problem has been re-opened and re-studied in light of its relevance to ecclesiology. Dom Paul De Vooght[20] regards the bull of Martin V, *Inter cunctas* (April 22, 1418) against the Hussites, as "a decisive argument in favor of the approbation of the conciliarist decrees" by the pope. In approving what had been done *conciliariter* at the council, the pope also approved of the conciliar Fifth Session; since approbation was extended to the council *simpliciter* and without distinction, it must have included the Fifth Session. For Dom De Vooght the *fact* of papal approval is beyond dispute. The problem is to determine the *quality* of this approval. "There is no question," he writes, "of the solemn approval by which the pope, inasmuch as he is sovereign pontiff, ratifies decisions taken by a council. The intervention of Martin V in this last session does not have this character . . . Because of the definitions recently promulgated, which placed the council above the pope, a papal ratification was scarcely conceivable at the mo-

[19] According to Cardinal d'Ailly the Roman Curia had agreed that the decrees on Conciliarism had not been solemnly approved by the Council because the Cardinals had not accepted them. But for him, as for others, the Cardinals were *the* successors of the apostles in their primary and primordial function. Thus he applied to them the words: "sunt cardines orbis terrae et posuit super eos orbem."

[20] P. De Vooght, "Le Conciliarisme aux conciles de Constance et de Bâle," *Le Concile et les Conciles* (Gembloux 1960), pp. 143–81, esp. p. 161; and, under the same title, 'Compléments et Précisions,' in *Irenikon* 36 (1963) 61–75, esp. p. 64.

ment . . ." Thus the pope ratified (though not solemnly) the conciliar decrees, probably no more than as part of a practical program to be followed for a time and later to be repudiated. This same historico-theological problem has also been handled by Hans Küng in his important contribution to ecclesiology, *Strukturen der Kirche*.[21] While generally accepting the conclusions of Dom De Vooght he goes further in maintaining that the mitigated Conciliarism of Constance, if rightly interpreted, can be harmonized with the papalism of the Vatican Council. Briefly, we have here two conciliar definitions of different orders which apply to two different sets of circumstances: Constance defining a conciliar superiority limited to extraordinary circumstances (e.g., in case of heresy of the pope, or the loss of his freedom), the Vatican defining the personal infallibility and primacy of the pope as the head of the ordinary *magisterium*. Each in its own way renders an indispensable service to the Church. The former is to provide for the extraordinary needs of the papacy, the latter for the ordinary and extraordinary needs of the Church.

Whether or not the Conciliarism of Constance was approved or repudiated, it remained in the theoretical order a dead letter as far as the Holy See itself was concerned. Martin V approved only of what had been done at Constance "in favorem fidei", and no theologian has held that Conciliarism, even of a mitigated nature, is "in favorem

---

[21] Quaestiones Disputatae 17 (Freiburg 1962) 244 ff. Obviously my remarks here on De Vooght and Küng are only intended to indicate the *drift* of their thought. In no sense am I presenting the fullness of their argumentation on this difficult question.

fidei." For the ecclesiology on which Conciliarism rested
made the papacy in the ultimate analysis irrelevant to the
Church, transformed it into a modified form of congrega-
tionalism or episcopalism. But papal disdain of erroneous
lines of thought does not extinguish them. The anti-papal
principles of the reform Council of Constance, like Pisa
before it and Basle after it, remained to plague the papacy
for decades, and absorbed time and energy which should
have been devoted to the renewal of the Church. The same
old problems remained, grew more and more complicated,
engendered new problems which spread over the entire
Christendom. As the century advanced, the Church became
like a jungle grown wild; and to the dismay of all truly sincere, religious men there was no one in sight with sufficient
strength and courage to apply the ax to the root of it all.[22]

On September 30, 1420, Pope Martin V entered Rome
amid the universal acclaim of his people. The long captivity of Avignon was finally over, the Great Schism successfully terminated, the papacy restored once more to its right-
ful home. The new pope had very wisely declined the invitation both of the emperor Sigismund to reside in Germany
and of the French king to return to Avignon. Rome was in
shambles, its churches and monuments in ruins, desolation
everywhere. The Leonine City with its deserted, prostrate
sanctuaries resembled a barren wasteland. Disease and
famine, poverty and hunger prevailed throughout the city
which once had been one of the wonders of the civilized
world. The remnant of the Roman clergy that came forth to

[22] Cf. Y. M. J. Congar, *Vraie et fausse réforme dans l'Eglise*
(Paris 1950), pp. 198 ff.

greet its bishop was ill clad and half starving. It was a city whose profound misery had been aptly described by St. Gregory the Great (d. 604) more than eight hundred years before in the dark days of the barbarians.[23] According to a contemporary report "by night, wolves came out of the desolate Campagna, invaded the Vatican Gardens, with their claws dug up the dead in the neighboring Campo Santo."[24] In a sense the decline and decay of the fabric of the city of Rome mirrored vividly the general moral collapse of Christendom.

In accord with the decree *Frequens* (October 9, 1417) of the Council of Constance the pope was committed to convoking a general council five years after its closure (April 22, 1418), then again seven years later, finally every ten years. The General Council, the foundation on which the Conciliarists rested their reform program, expressed their sacred conviction that what the pope could not or would not do in the matter of reforming the Church, a council both could and would achieve. In accord with the expressed wishes of the Fathers of Constance, Martin convoked a Council to meet at Pavia in the spring of 1423. Despite the dread which even the mention of the word council filled him, despite his personal aversion to the principles of Conciliarism, Martin was faithful to his commitment.[25]

The surprisingly small number of prelates who appeared at the opening date of the General Council of Pavia on April 23, 1423 demonstrated how quickly the primitive en-

[23] *Hom in Ezech.* 2, Hom. 6, 22–24 (PL 76, 1009–1012).
[24] Cf. L. Pastor, *op. cit.*, 1, 216.
[25] *Ibid.*, 1, 238, 280.

thusiasm for conciliar reform had vanished.[26] When the plague invaded the city in the early summer of that year, the council transferred to Siena, presumably free from pestilence and readily accessible to the pope, who, of course, did not appear. Finally, in November, the first session was held; subsequent sessions witnessed endless debate on a variety of side issues; in March of the following year it closed. Considered from the point of view of general reform, it was a total failure, for it lacked both the will and the conviction to take up this great work which, if accomplished in a thorough fashion, would surely have proved the undoing of many a prelate who attended this pathetic synod.[27]

The Council of Pavia-Siena failed. Already the first quarter of the fifteenth century had been reached. Two reform councils had met. Decrees had been published. But the *status quo* had remained unaltered. The blame for this negligence must be pinned on Martin V[28] whose small interest in the problem of reformation can be measured by his refusal

[26] Cf. Hefele-Leclercq, *op. cit.*, 7, 1, 613: "It is rather astonishing that there was not present at the council any prelate of the Italian nation (save for the presidents). This is hardly explicable, if the pope seriously envisioned the success of the council."

[27] At least one ecclesiastic, Jerome of Florence, O.P., had the courage to dress down the conciliar Fathers: "A General Council," he said, "is not indispensable for the reform of the Church. Too many councils end by weakening the papacy. Sinners, wicked men, cannot assemble in the name of Jesus Christ . . ." For this blast he was threatened with arrest by the Fathers. Cf. Hefele-Leclercq, *op. cit.*, 7, 1. 631.

[28] P. Hughes, *op. cit.*, 3, 319, n. 2; Hefele-Leclercq, *op. cit.*, 7, 1, 644, and L. Pastor, *op. cit.*, 1, 238–40 agree in fixing the blame on Martin. There seems no doubt that his irresponsible policy was rooted in a stubborn refusal to heed, or even listen to, the advice of people better informed than himself. Cf. L. Pastor, *op. cit.*, 1, 263.

to lend the prestige of his presence to the faltering Council of Siena and by the insipid reform program, which he outlined in the spring of 1425, a program concerned for the most part with the most irrelevant aspects of ecclesiastical life. Once again all clerics from the highest to the lowest level, including even the servants of the cardinals, are reminded of their obligation to wear the proper dress; prelates, in addition to avoiding concubinage, are to avoid wearing red or green clothing; and those clerics, who accompany them, should not be outfitted as squires.[29] This obviously was getting at the heart of the problem!

In compliance with the prescriptions of the Fathers of Siena, Martin convoked a General Council to meet at Basle which would be the sixteenth ecumenical council in the history of the Church. Before it assembled, the pope had died of apoplexy on February 20, 1431. His successor, Eugene IV, Gabriele Condulmaro of Venice, was elected on March 2nd, but not before he had sworn in the Conclave to observe a 'capitulation' which pledged him to retain the Curia in Rome, to observe the prescriptions of Constance in naming cardinals, and to summon a council to reform the Church in head and members.[30] But the duplicity of the cardinals, who proposed this 'capitulation,' is revealed in the fact that they "required that he should make no concession which could be prejudicial to the papal dignity or to the Roman Court." This meant, of course, no reform. On March 11th the new pope was consecrated and solemnly crowned; on the following day in obedience to his solemn

29 Cf. Hefele-Leclercq, op. cit., 7, 1, 645–46.
30 Cf. L. Pastor, op. cit., 1, 284.

promise to his electors, he approved the convocation of the Council of Basle, which was to torment him for years to come. In fact, his entire pontificate was destined to be absorbed in a fight to death with the forces of radical Conciliarism which formed the backbone of this notorious, antipapal council.

On December 14, 1431, the first public session of the Council of Basle, with only a handful of bishops and abbots in attendance, was held in the cathedral church of St. Leonard. The Council was under the presidency of the papal legate, Cardinal Julian Cesarini, who had just returned from Germany whither he had been sent by Eugene to organize and launch a crusade against the Hussites. The crushing, humiliating defeat of the Catholics,[31] which he witnessed on August 14th of that year, was vivid in his mind when he arrived at Basle; and he hoped, therefore, that this Council would find a more reasonable method of reconciling the Bohemian heretics to the Church. His personal experience in Germany had made him a realist with eyes wide open to the grave crisis which was developing in Central Europe. After Mass had been solemnly celebrated before the Fathers of the Council, he addressed them on the triple purpose (a triad to be repeated over and over again until Trent, a century later) for which they had been gathered together: the extirpation of heresy, the reestablishment of peace among Christian nations, and the reform of the Church in head and members.[32]

[31] Both the papal bull decreeing the crusade and the papal standard were captured by the Hussites.

[32] Cf. Hefele-Leclercq, op. cit., 7, 2, 692–93.

A few days later, the papal nuncio, Daniel of Panenzo, arrived with a special papal bull (*Quoniam alto*, dated Dec. 18, 1431) in which pope Eugene had decreed the dissolution of the Council—four days after it had opened! But face to face with the Fathers of the Council the nuncio seems to have lacked the courage either to promulgate this bull or even to admit that he had been dispatched to Basle for this precise purpose.[33] Only some weeks later, on January 13, 1432, after Daniel had quietly departed for Strasbourg, John Ceparelli of Prato, a young doctor of the papal nuncio's entourage, dared to read the bull of dissolution which was to bring the council to an abrupt end. The announcement of this peculiar decision, greeted with the deepest resentment, was symptomatic of the disobedience and rebellion which would characterize the whole subsequent history of the Council's relations with Eugene.[34] The pope's bull was "a grievous mistake, prematurely revealing his extreme distrust of the Council, before any act or decision of that body had occurred to justify it."[35]

In view of the fact that pope Eugene was thoroughly acquainted with the past twenty-five years of Church history, his procedure is difficult to understand. For surely he must have known that the whole of fifteenth century conciliar thought and action smoldered with insubordination, mis-

[33] In all fairness it must be admitted that the role of Daniel at Basle and his relations to Cardinal Cesarini and the Council are not altogether clear.

[34] Cf. P. Hughes, *The Church in Crisis* (New York 1960), p. 275: "The history of the reign of Eugene IV is, in one respect, little more than the history of the Council of Basle."

[35] Cf. L. Pastor, *op. cit.*, 1, 287.

trust, and pretensions to independence of the Holy See; and that the Fathers at Basle would have to be managed with finesse, if a crisis were to be avoided. Obviously Eugene (now partly paralyzed) was seriously misinformed or uninformed on the true character of the Council which he saw fit to dissolve. Did he really expect that these prelates, steeped in Conciliarism and well informed on the right and privileges which Constance had conferred upon the Council, would quietly and in orderly fashion depart from Basle because the pope had spoken? If he did, the history of the following decade shows how thoroughly he had been deceived.

On February 2nd in the second session, the Fathers of the Council—now gathered not only without papal approval but in bold defiance of it—gave the pope sixty days in which to withdraw his bull of dissolution. In fact, on August 20th the Council informed him in clearest terms that it alone could dissolve itself and that it alone enjoyed infallibility. In the General Congregation of September 3, 1431, the Fathers made their mind very clear and explicit in replying to an address delivered by John of Tarentum in defense of the papal prerogatives:[36]

We render to His Holiness what is due to him. Let him ever render to the universal Church what is her due, by recognizing the authority of the General Council, according to the decrees of

[36] John, Archbishop of Tarente and papal plenipotentiary, had been sent by Eugene to the Council with the hope that an *entente* might be established between pope and Council. His discourse on the papacy, delivered on August 23, 1432, held up monarchical government in the Church as the most perfect government, on the basis of authority (Aristotle and St. Thomas) and the order of nature itself. Cf. Hefele-Leclercq, *op. cit.*, 7, 2, 743 ff.

the Council of Constance. . . . The Roman Pontiff himself is bound to obey the mandates, the statutes, the ordinations and the precepts of the holy synod of Basle and of every other General Council that has been legitimately convoked, in those matters which pertain to the extirpation of schism and the general reform of the Church of God in head and members, in accord with the decrees of the Council of Florence, representing the Catholic Church. . . .[37]

There was no question here of an outright negation of the divine origin of the papacy and its primatial place in the whole Church. But this truth, superficially admitted by almost all, had been so manipulated and distinguished by the Conciliarists as to have received a meaning in almost direct contradiction to the traditional sense in which the words had been understood. The position of the pope in this ecclesiology was "very great, but no greater than the whole Church," which the General Council must and does concretely represent. The issue turned on the character of the relation of the pope to the Council, and of the Council to the Church. The Fathers of Basle had every intention of reducing theoretical Conciliarism to the practical order, and in the year 1432 it seemed as if there was no one in the Church sufficiently strong to halt their march.

In December, 1432 the Council demanded not only that Eugene withdraw his bull of dissolution of December 18, 1431 but also that he solemnly approve all that the Council had accomplished up to the present. At the tenth session on February 19, 1433 the pope was declared contumacious. Sixty days had already passed since the promulgation of the

[37] J. Mansi, *Sacrorum conciliorum nova et amplissima collectio* 29, 245.

Council's ultimatum, and he had taken no steps towards implementing its demand for the withdrawal of the bull of dissolution. Accordingly canonical process was instituted against the pope. On April 27th more anti-papal legislation issued from the Council.[38] On July 13th, in the twelfth session, it deprived the Holy See forever of its right to name bishops, abbots and other dignitaries—a decree to whose observance every future pope was to bind himself by an inviolable oath—and it also demanded once again that Eugene withdraw his detested bull of dissolution. Without knowledge of these proceedings Eugene had already promulgated another bull (*Inscrutabilis*) on July 29th which not only defended the rights of the Holy See against the Council but also nullified all the acts of the Council against it. In addition a scathing denunciation was pronounced against the Council as working ". . . to the great and evident prejudice of the Church and the Apostolic See, a grave scandal to many. . . ." a Council ordered "not to reformation, but deformation, not to unity but to the rupture of the Church, not to removing heresy but nurturing it, not the peace of the faithful but to sowing discord. . . ."[39]

A few days later, on August 1st, Eugene by his celebrated bull, *Dudum sacrum*, completely reversed his whole policy in dealing with the Council. Now he agrees and willingly accepts (*volumus et contantamur*) both the legitimate existence of the Council since its opening, and it future existence, all as if no modification, dissolution or transference had taken place! In fact, he formally retracted its transfer-

[38] Hefele-Leclercq, *op. cit.*, 7, 2, 799 ff.
[39] J. Mansi, *op. cit.*, 29, 80.

ence to Bologna, provided for by the bull, *Quoniam alto*, on December 18th of the previous year, and declared further his simple, open and cordial adherence to the Council which he will in the future sustain with all his power. As a last stroke of diplomacy, he added the condition, "that Our legates be admitted with every respect to the presidency of the Council, and that each and every fact and deed against Our person, authority and liberty, and that of the Apostolic See . . . be removed, and that everything be returned to its former state. And thus with one mind and one spirit, with charity and purity let the Council proceed with its business."[40] It goes without saying that the Fathers at Basle saw in this very humble submission toleration rather than approbation. It was flatly rejected and their outrageous demands reiterated.

While the pope was preparing another general abrogation of all the anti-papal decrees of the Council, he suddenly found himself in the position of a fugitive, generally deserted and scarcely in a position to duel with Basle. Under the leadership of "the very soul of all antipapal conspiracies," Philip Maria Visconti, the hostile Milanese had invaded the papal states and Eugene was forced to flee in panic to Florence. It was from here on December 15, 1433, that he issued yet another bull named *Dudum sacrum*, a frank admission that his act of dissolution had caused grave trouble, and a total submission to the most anti-papal demands of the Council. This bull has rightly been characterized as "the nadir of papal action."[41]

[40] *Ibid.*, 29, 574; Hefele-Leclercq, *op. cit.*, 7, 2, 814.
[41] P. Hughes, *The Church in Crisis*, p. 277. Cf. also J. Gill, *Eugenius IV. Pope of Christian Union* (Westminster 1961), p. 58, who refers to the *Dudum sacrum* as "a complete surrender."

Until 1449 the Council of Basle continued in existence, each year losing more and more of its prestige and dragging Conciliarism deeper and deeper into the mud with it. These sixteen years (1433–49) are pages of history filled with the same old tactics; anti-papal decrees, outbursts of sensitivity, petty wrangling and fighting, farcical theatrics, and general irresponsibility. If this represented Conciliarism at work, surely no one would take it very seriously. After October 1437 the moderate party under Cardinal Cesarini deserted Basle for Ferrara whither Eugene had convoked a new Council to deal with the important Greek question of union, which was now coming to the fore. On June 25, 1439 the Council, composed at this time of what must be considered the lunatic fringe of Christendom under Cardinal d'Allemand, deposed Eugene IV and elected Amadeus of Savoy who took the name Felix V. The petty relations between this last anti-pope and this last schismatical council only served to alienate all the important friends upon whom the council could once count. It held its last session at Basle on May 16, 1443, then transferred to Lausanne, where Felix was 'holding court,' and finally on April 25, 1449 breathed its last.

One half of the fifteenth century had already run its course. The Church had still hesitated before the work of reform. The cancer, difformatio, left to itself, continued to grow and spread on all levels. In England the fierce anti-papal Lollard movement was gradually consolidating its influence. The teaching of Wycliff had found fertile soil in which to grow; and in Bohemia, the problem, 'solved' by the unfortunate burning of John Hus, was reaching dangerous proportions—expanding, in fact, far out beyond the area of purely theological discussion into open and violent bloodshed. The crusade of Martin V against the Bohemian heretics had accomplished nothing more than to humiliate the Holy See while uniting those, whom he wished to convert, into a vast anti-papal army. And the perennial Turkish menace was burying its roots deep into European soil. The venerable Byzantine empire was ready to topple down before this unchristian power and bring to a close more than a thousand years of history. The delicate, and highly important, question of the union of the Greeks and Rome was pressing for a satisfactory and permanent solution; and, as always, there was the matter of reform of the Church in head and members.

There is probably no factor in the fifteenth century which demonstrates better than the ecumenical councils themselves the futility to which Conciliarism could bring the whole reform program of the Church. The Council of Constance failed not only because it deviated from the apostolic constitution of the Church but also because its plans for reform were neither realistically conceived nor actually implemented. The Council of Pavia-Siena, apart from the fact that it never really came to maturity, achieved nothing of a lasting character for the cause of reform. For it never received from either the papacy or the episcopacy that full measure of confidence and support without which no ecumenical synod can effectively operate. The Council of Basle only proved how hopeless reform must necessarily be when it is separated from faith and obedience, from the essential ingredients of Catholicism as the Church of Christ on earth.

In many respects the Council of Basle is the scandal par *excellence* of the pre-Reformation Church, for it demonstrated in a way more concrete, vivid, and cogent than any theoretist could have done it, that if the papacy would not reform the Church neither would any council in rebellion against it. The bold, subversive, schismatical attitude of this Council, especially its anti-papal decrees, destroyed its authority in Christendom and weakened the prestige of the papacy at a time when it should have been the cornerstone of the reform movement. By branding the Holy See as the source of all evil in the Church and as an institution incapable of providing for the Church, this contumacious Council created the atmosphere most beneficial to the growth and development of anti-papalism; and by publicly exposing to common abuse and defilement the Roman See, "the head and mother of Christendom," it disturbed deeply the piety and reverence of the laity. For it accustomed the ordinary simple Christian to lawlessness and rebellion in the name of religion by inviting him to witness the spectacle of an assembly of churchmen in revolution against their sovereign head, and by asking him to join a schism instigated and presided over by the foremost prelates in the Church. The distance which separates rebellion *in* the Church from rebellion *against* the Church is always slender. History has proved this over and over again.

In view of the manifold crises which beset the Church in these dark days, the absorption of ecclesiastical administrators in side issues is reprehensible. Their irresponsible attitude toward the questions which were posed on all sides, their refusal to face and solve the great reform problem, only raised more questions and problems that were still harder to solve. The way to the great revolution of the following century opened wider and clearer. With the rejection of Basle, Conciliarism ceased to be a living issue; but, at the same time, it was clear to all that the work of reform, now needed more badly than ever, could not be entrusted to a Council. The Holy See had secured a notable and deserved victory over the opposition of the anti-papal. forces. It remained now for the papacy itself to demonstrate to the world that it would indeed reform the Church by removing all those ugly abuses, those administrative, theological, and moral deficiencies whose existence had become a crying scandal to Christendom; and that it would seriously work for the renewal of the hearts and minds of men through whose restoration to the image of God the true reform of the Church can alone be realized.

IV

THE PAPACY (1417–1517)

The Council of Basle, convoked in 1431, was transferred to
Ferrara in 1438, and finally dispersed in 1449, the same
year in which Felix V, the last anti-pope in the history
of the Church withdrew his ridiculous claim.[1] The Great
Schism had ended, and the papacy had definitely con-
quered Conciliarism, in fact for all practical purposes had
securely buried it. It would never pose the dangerous threat
of Constance and Basle. Despite the disturbed state of the
late medieval world, which seemed well on the way to its
dissolution, the Church had weathered the storm. Peace
and union had been established in Western Christendom;
and there was even the bright prospect of reunion with
the separated Oriental churches (Florence, July 6, 1449).[2]
At the coronation of Nicholas V in 1447, ambassadors from
all parts of Europe promised their national obediences;

[1] After his resignation he was named Cardinal of St. Sabina by
the generous pope Nicholas and made Apostolic Vicar-general for
several dioceses. He was even provided for financially. He died January 7, 1451.
[2] Cf. on the important Council of Florence and the union of the
Orientals with the Latins, J. Gill, The Council of Florence (Cambridge 1959).

and, three years later, the vast throng of pilgrims that flocked to Rome for the Jubilee gave clear testimony to the common man's acceptance and reverence of the papacy.[3] The intellectual atmosphere of the day with its spirit of rebirth and discovery suggested interesting new developments in art, literature, spirituality, and even theology. The Church was not without her saints and scholars.[4] And towards the end of the century the discovery of America would open the New World to the old faith.

But in the one hundred and fifty years since Clement V had established the papacy at Avignon, its juridical, moral, and religious position had suffered seriously from neglect, scandal, and abuse. The dignity of the Holy See had indeed been offended, but it was still respected; and would be more solidly respected, if it were spiritually restored. In view of the fact that Eugene IV had already initiated the preliminary phases of this renewal, the middle of the fifteenth century might have been a turning point in the history of the papacy's exaltation.[5] But the seventy years be-

[3] The Holy Year was intended to be a solemn occasion for the exaltation of the Holy See. After the Council of Constance, Martin V (and the following popes) concentrated more on the temporal restoration of the papacy than its spiritual. Among other factors the financial, as always in this period, was of prime importance. Cf. P. Partner, The Papal State under Martin V (London 1958), pp. 42–94.

[4] For example, St. Joan of Arc (d. 1431), St. Bernardine of Siena (d. 1444), St. John Capistrano (d. 1456) and St. Antoninus of Florence (d. 1459). Among the ecclesiastical scholars of the day can be mentioned Nicholas of Cusa (d. 1464), Juan de Torquemada (d. 1468) and Cardinal Bessarion (d. 1472).

[5] Cf. the evaluation of Eugene IV in L. Pastor, The History of the Popes 1, 352: "When he died, the men of most importance were on the side of Rome. The opponents of the Apostolic See and of the

tween 1447 and 1517, far from showing clear signs of a
spiritual transformation of the Holy See, form a regrettable
chapter in its history, a scandal, which remains to plague us
even to this day. What was lacking at this critical moment
was distinguished, capable, courageous, responsible leadership in the Church, rare qualities for which there are no
adequate substitutes this side of the miraculous.

Eugene IV died at Rome on February 23, 1447 after a
reign of sixteen years. Some weeks later, on March 6th, he
was succeeded by the pious, peace-loving, cultivated Nicholas V (Tommaso Parentucelli),[6] who is known in history
as the first pope of the Renaissance, "the first papal
patron of literature and the fine arts."[7] It is part of the
cruelty of history that the Church, which sighed for a reformer, received as its head a humanist, a Christian humanist indeed, but one filled with more than a little sympathy
for the neo-pagan culture of his day. His admiration of the
new art poured over into full support of the Renaissance,
now just dawning in Rome; and his generous patronage and
protection liberally extended to humanists such as Poggio
Bracciolini, Lorenzo Valla, Giannozzo Manetti and Gio-

monarchical constitution of the Church, in short all the anti-
ecclesiastical elements, had sustained a notable defeat. The attempt
to change the Pope into a mere phantom ruler, a sort of Doge, had
come to nought."

[6] Despite the traditional antagonism of the Colonnas and the
Orsinis the election of Nicholas V was above petty politics. "Truly
in this election," wrote the Sienese ambassador, "God has manifested His power, which surpasses all human prudence and wisdom."
Cf. L. Pastor, op. cit., 2, 12.

[7] L. Pastor gives this title to the volume (2, 1) of his work which
handles the pontificate of Nicholas V.

vanni Tortello, and to artists such as Antonio Averulino, Leon Battista Alberti and countless others who found in the pope a sincere admirer and lavish patron of their art.[8] Under Nicholas the Rome of the Middle Ages became the Rome of the Renaissance.

The Jubilee Year, 1450, was a year of papal triumph. For the first time in one hundred and fifty years, since the Jubilee of Boniface VIII in 1300, a pope was able to celebrate the Holy Year in Rome conscious that he stood at the head of a united Christendom. The atmosphere of the city was filled with the spirit of the restored papacy and the highest hopes were expressed on all sides for a rapid reformation of the Universal Church. Countless Holy Year pilgrims of all classes and of all nations streamed into the Eternal City to visit the tombs of Sts. Peter and Paul and to gain the coveted Jubilee indulgence. The fervor of their faith, enthusiasm, and ardour before the great shrines of Christendom were a living testimonial to the confidence which the simple faithful had in the Holy See. They marvelled at the magnificent, new edifices which were to be seen on all sides, and the splendid new churches, filled with the new art and beauty of the Renaissance artists. But they failed to see the ominous shadows of disaster which lurked behind this majestic façade; and had they seen these dark shadows, it is not very likely that they would have understood the boding reality which they symbolized.

Nicholas V was not the sort of churchman to undertake

[8] His prodigal lavishness (in the midst of much poverty) in support of artists and his lack of discernment in selecting his personal entourage were almost scandalous.

the vast revolutionary enterprise which true reformation involved. By natural disposition he was inclined more to the development of the esthetic than the moral or the theological.[9] He was above all peace-loving, a quality which does not harmonize with the spirit of reformation. Thus he preferred to play the role of Maecenas; and without ever taking a significant share in renewing the life of the Church, he became deeply engrossed in the active, generous support of the art and literature of the Renaissance. It is in this direction that the real importance of his pontificate lies. "In lending the resources and authority of the Holy See to the promotion of learning and art, he inaugurated a new era both in the history of the Papacy and in that of culture."[10] But in thus engaging the Church, in diverting her from her true mission in this world, he bears a real responsibility before history which expected so much from him. In seriously neglecting the reform of the Church which was entrusted to him as its chief bishop he neglected her where the need was greatest; and left, thereby, the door open wide to the revolutionary reformers of the following century.

Nicholas' deficiency in this whole area of the pastoral is not to be explained by lack of good will or personal sanctity on his part. It was rather that he was neither fully aware of the true state of the Church nor appreciative of the extent to which the scandals and disturbances of the previous centuries were working serious damage. He did at-

---

[9] He has been described as "a well informed dilettante wandering at will wherever his fancy led him." Cf. L. Pastor, op. cit., 2, 22.

[10] Cf. L. Pastor, op. cit., 2, 165.

tempt reform; but his half hearted attempt, however excellent in itself, shows a misconception of both means and end. It was neither universal nor thorough, and though inspired by good will, accomplished very little.[11] Had Nicholas surrounded himself, as did the reforming popes of the late eleventh century, with the outstanding churchmen of the day, with those who thoroughly appreciated the spiritual needs of the Church and who could best devise ways and means of renewing her in this hour of crisis, his pontificate would most certainly have turned in a different direction.[12] Preoccupied with humanism and the humanists, Nicholas did not fully grasp the significance of his obligation as pope to provide for the general welfare of the *Ecclesia universalis*. His contribution here would have been significant, if the attention, which he had devoted to the interests of his family, had been directed towards the formation of the College of Cardinals into a group of expert and cooperative advisers, an advisory cabinet devoted to the interests of the universal Church.

Viewed purely from esthetic considerations, Nicholas V's extraordinary patronage of art and literature, his foundation of the Vatican Library, his extensive (but colossal and worldly) plans for the rebuilding of the Vatican Borgo, the papal palace and St. Peter's Church merit him a distinguished place in the history of Western culture. But in

[11] The most serious reform-effort at this time was the work of the German Cardinal Nicholas of Cusa, papal legate to Germany, in 1451. Cf. the glowing tribute paid to this saintly churchman by Trithemius cited in L. Pastor, *op. cit.*, 2, 137. However, not even this tireless worker could solve the vast German problem.

[12] Side by side with cardinals such as Nicholas of Cusa, Juan de Carvajal and Juan de Torquemada, we find Barbo, Scarampa and d'Estouteville.

virtue of his sacred office as Christ's Vicar and supreme
head of the Church, serious doubts arise about the value
of this pretentious enterprise. For his deep involvement in
esthetics, especially the new pagan *belles lettres*, not only
distracted him from the pressing religious issues of the day
but led him to foster the spirit of the Renaissance with its
indifference to Christianity, sympathy for the ideals of
pagan antiquity (its morality as well as its art forms), and
serious neglect of the sacred and the religious.[13] Joined to
this *Weltanschauung*, so alien to true religion, was that
secular spirit which, in its disregard of the supernatural
character of Christianity, was destined to eat into the very
entrails of the Church.[14]

In justice to Nicholas it should be pointed out that his
extraordinary plans to embellish Rome were not inspired by
personal vanity, but by considerations of "the exaltation of
the power of the Holy See throughout Christendom." According to this very modern concept of propaganda, the more
magnificent the externals of the Roman Church, the deeper
the reverence, awe and respect which they would inspire
among "the uncultured masses." The majesty of papal
Rome, its exaltation and *triumphalismus* were to parallel
the power of pagan Rome.[15] And all this vast program of
aggrandizement would lead to the enlargement of the dig-

[13] Though Nicholas was essentially a Christian humanist, his close
association with the Renaissance unconsciously involved him in certain pagan aspects of it.

[14] For example, Poggio Bracciolini, "one of the most repulsive
figures of the period," one of its most immoral authors, and Lorenzo
Valla, author of *On Pleasure* (1431), which is "nothing but Epi-
cureanism pure and simple," were both befriended by Nicholas.
Other examples could be cited.

[15] Cf. L. Pastor, *op. cit.*, 2, 165 ff.

nity and the authority of the Holy See. But it is interesting
to note with Manetti, the pope's biographer, that of the
five major projects, which Nicholas had at heart, "all great
and important works," none directly touched on reform,
but were concerned with artistic construction.[16]

Weighed down with deep anxiety over the fate of Christendom, especially in the dark days after the fall of Con-
stantinople in 1453, Nicholas died on March 25, 1455. At
the end, on his death bed, he prayed before the cardinals:
"Almighty God, give the Holy Church a pastor who will
uphold her and make her increase." The body of the dead
pope, who has been represented as "the light and the or-
nament of God's Church and of his age," was laid to rest in
St. Peter's basilica.[17]

The conclave, which assembled in Rome on April 4,
1455 to find a successor to Nicholas V, passed over the
distinguished cardinals Capranica and Bessarion[18] to elect
Alfonso de Borgia, Archbishop of Valencia, Spaniard, re-
nowned jurist and experienced diplomat, who took the
name Callixtus III.[19] He was a man of blameless character: pious, studious, serious minded, temperate, dignified,
unmoved by flattery, independent. Unlike his predecessor,
he was not a man of the Renaissance, had little sympathy for

[16] Ibid., 2, 169.

[17] Ibid., 2, 313.

[18] Note the insolent remark made in the conclave by Alain of
Avignon: "Shall we give the Latin Church a neophyte and Greek as
pope? Bessarion has not yet shaved his beard, and shall he be our
head?" Cf. F. Gregorovius, History of the City of Rome in the
Middle Ages 7, 1 (London 1909), 149.

[19] Callixtus, believing that his election to the papacy had been
prophesied by Vincent Ferrer, canonized him on June 29, 1455.
This was one of the first acts of his pontificate.

the new humanism, evaluated learning from a practical viewpoint, and questioned the true worth of the whole artistic undertaking of his predecessor.[20]

The best energies of his pontificate were devoted to honoring and furthering his worthless nephews and organizing and launching a vast crusade against the menace of Islam. In the gradual penetration of Islam into Europe, especially into Serbia and Hungary, Callixtus rightly detected a peril which would most certainly consume Western Christendom, if allowed to spread unchecked; and it was his firm resolve to check this growing threat at every stage. Despite the general indifference with which the Western World viewed the formidable situation which confronted it, Callixtus used every means, even the alienation of the property of the Church, to raise a crusade army for the defense and protection of Christendom. The great saving victory on July 14, 1456, when the Hungarian hero John Hunyadi successfully repelled the Turks before the walls of Belgrade, must be considered a personal victory of Pope Callixtus, for he, more than any prince in Christendom, had organized this victorious Christian army, and supported it at very great personal inconvenience.

The crusade idea mastered the pontificate of Callixtus. All the resources of the Church were expended on this project. All the energies of the pope were directed to the end that a crusade army be raised and dispatched to those parts of Europe most afflicted by Islam. The threat was

[20] F. Gregorovius (op. cit., 7, 1, 151) has given us this caricature of the pope: "His short reign was devoid of importance. The Vatican resembled an infirmary, where the gouty Pope spent the greater part of his time by candle-light in bed, surrounded by nephews or mendicant monks."

real and pressing. No one can seriously criticize Callixtus' efforts in this direction. The only regret is that these military feats which properly belonged to the temporal lords of Christendom, especially to the Holy Roman Emperor, fell by default to the Holy See. The most immediate result of this deep involvement in the crusade was the directing of papal interest toward the East, far from Italy and the Renaissance, but also far from Rome and reform. Little energy and few resources remained for this latter highly urgent task.

Of Pope Callixtus it has been said that "the only blot on his otherwise blameless character" was his "excessive nepotism,"[21] his shocking favoritism to his ill-deserving nephews, Luis Juan de Mila and Rodrigo Lançol.[22] Both were recipients at his hands of most extraordinary gifts, benefices, and preferments which were totally unmerited. Both were created cardinals[23] though neither contributed their spiritual and temporal resources to the well-being of the Church through whose generosity they were prospering. Both were immoral, irresponsible scoundrels who used the papacy in the person of their aged uncle for their own self-centered purposes. They were insolent, proud young men, arrogant creators of ill will and scandal wherever they presented themselves. "Could Callixtus have foreseen that his blind affection for his nephews was to render the hitherto stainless name of his family a synonym for all infamy in the

---

[21] Cf. L. Pastor, op. cit., 2, 447.

[22] The third nephew, Don Pedro Luis, brother of Rodrigo, did not embrace the clerical state. He was honored with the Dukedom of Spoleto. All three nephews took their uncle's family name, Borgia.

[23] This was done in clear defiance of the Capitulation which Callixtus had sworn to uphold at his election.

history of the Church, it is probable that he would have banished the sons of his four sisters to the darkest dungeons of Spain."[24] Their sordid history cannot be fully reproduced here. It is sufficient to say that Rodrigo Borgia, cardinal at twenty-five years of age, later ascended the papal throne to take the notorious name of Alexander VI.

The extravagant nepotism of this Spanish pope and his undisguised favoritism to his greedy countrymen (the Catalans) only served to increase the Italian mistrust of foreign influence in the papacy. Thus the conclave which assembled after the death of Callixtus, after certain hesitations,[25] elected Aeneas Silvius Piccolomini on August 19, 1458, who significantly took the name Pius II.[26] He was a native Italian, a man of considerable experience, personally acquainted with the Church in northern Europe, a devoted churchman, large minded, hostile to abuse of which he was

[24] Cf. F. Gregorovius, op. cit., 7, 1, 156.

[25] The eight Italian cardinals in the conclave equated the election of an Italian pope with the honor of the Church. Thus Piccolomini addressed the cardinal of Pavia: "A French pope will either go to France—and then our dear country is bereft of its splendor; or he will stay among us—and Italy, the queen of nations, will serve a foreign master, while we shall be the slaves of the French. . . . You now have to chose whether you prefer to betray Italy, your country, and the Church or the bishop of Rouen." The Commentaries of Pius II, tr. F. A. Gragg, Smith College Studies in History 22, 1–2 (1937) 99–100.

[26] The name Pius was inspired by Vergil's Pius Aeneas. Significant is Cardinal d'Estouteville's evaluation of Piccolomini: "What is Aeneas to you? Why do you think him worthy of the papacy? Will you give us a lame, poverty stricken pope? How shall a destitute pope restore a destitute church, or an ailing pope an ailing church? He has recently come from Germany. We do not know him. Perhaps he will even transfer the Curia thither. . . . Shall we set a poet in Peter's place? Shall we govern the church by the laws of the heathen?" Ibid., p. 95.

well aware,[27] and conscious of the need for thorough reform. Like his predecessor he was overwhelmed—exces-
sively so—with the urgency of a crusade which would
achieve a definitive victory over the Turk, totally liberate
Europe from this menace, and rescue finally and restore
the holy places to the Christians. The most touching testimonial to the good will and sincerity of Pius II was his
willingness to be invested with the crusader's cross and his expressed wish personally to lead the crusade army to victory.
He died at Ancona on August 14, 1464 without having seen
the realization of his dream, a victim to his own generous
zeal poured out on what was surely a lost cause.

From the pontificate of Pius II date two highly interesting documents on reform—the work of Cardinal Nicholas of Cusa and Domenico de' Domenichi—prepared at
the request of the pope himself out of consideration of the
Capitulation Act of 1458.[28] The words, which the pope
addressed to the reform commission on the occasion of its
appointment, held out the great promise of renovation.
"Two things are particularly near my heart, the war with
the Turks, and the reform of the Roman Court. The
amendment of the whole state of ecclesiastical affairs, which
I have determined to undertake, depends on this Court
as its model. I purpose to begin by improving the morals of
the ecclesiastics here, and banishing all simony and other
abuses from hence."[29] The final sentence clearly definies
the method.

[27] Before his election he wrote: "There is nothing to be obtained
from the Roman Curia without money." Cf. F. Gregorovius, *op.
cit.*, 7, 1, 171.
[28] Cf. L. Pastor, *op. cit.*, 3, 10–11.
[29] *Ibid.*, 3, 269–70.

The reform programs which the two churchmen produced show a thorough grasp of the difficult problem which was to be solved.[30] Both produced a saving formula. Both boldly traced the root cause of the universal moral decadence to the Roman Curia; both accurately listed the prevalent abuses; both urged a systematic reform of the entire Church in head and members. Neither was motivated by human respect or personal gain. Cardinal Cusa's insistence on the guarantee of liberty of speech face to face with scandalous abuse, even in the Head of the Church, is significant. It shows a rare courage in handling a sensitive problem. The scheme which de' Domenichi proposed, with its division into twenty-two parts touching on all aspects of Roman clerical life, is equally courageous and thorough.[31]

Had the reform programs of these two churchmen been fully implemented, the subsequent development of the Church would certainly have moved rapidly in a different direction. For we have here the reform program of Trent in embryo. But for all practical purposes, apart from half-hearted measures, reform remained a dead letter. Thus Pastor writes of Pius II that ". . . he did not venture to engage in a gigantic conflict with all the evils which had invaded the Church, and contented himself with opposing isolated abuses . . . The question of reform was driven more and more into the background, and in the interests of the Church, this cannot be sufficiently regretted."[32]

Paul II (Pietro Barbo), nephew of Eugene IV, was

[30] Both programs were universal, thorough, and concrete in their aims. The reform was to reach from head to lowest members.

[31] Cf. L. Pastor, op. cit., 3, 270–75 where the two programs are summarized.

[32] Ibid., 3, 275.

elected August 30, 1464, and died seven years later, July 26, 1471, after an uneventful pontificate mostly dedicated to trifles.[33] But this vain *bon vivant*, so devoted to the Renaissance had the good sense to detect its pagan aspects and to take stern, decisive measures against it—the suppression of the Roman Academy and the College of Abbreviatores —which brought down upon him the wrath and the ill will of the humanists. The intense resentment which these peremptory measures roused expressed itself most cogently in the slanderous calumnies against the pope whose character remains defiled even to this day.[34]

Paul II died suddenly on July 26, 1471. Fifteen days later Francesco Cardinal della Rovere emerged from the conclave as Sixtus IV. Sprung from a poor, obscure family in Savona, this Franciscan friar had risen high in his fifty-seven years. He had been successful lecturer in sacred theology, distinguished Mariologist,[35] Minister General of the Friars Minor and finally, in 1467, Cardinal of the Church. He was competent, able, cultivated, and his personal life

[33] Preaching before the conclave which was to elect Paul II, Cardinal de' Domenichi outlined some of the problems which the new pope would have to solve: "The dignity of the Church must be reasserted, her authority revived, morals reformed, the Court regulated, the course of justice secured, the faith propagated, captives set free, lost cities regained, and the faithful armed for the Holy War." Almost none of this was accomplished by Pope Paul.

[34] This vilification was largely the work of Bartolomeo Platina (d. 1481) in his *Liber de vita Christi ac de vitiis summorum pontificum omnium* (Venice 1479). Despite his calumnies of the Holy See he was made librarian of the Vatican by Sixtus IV.

[35] As a theologian, Sixtus showed a certain originality in reconciling the teachings of Scotus and Aquinas on the Immaculate Conception. As pope, he issued two important constitutions, *Cum Praeexcelsa* (February 28, 1476), and *Grave Nimis* (September 4, 1483), on Marian doctrine.

was above reproach. His patronage of art is amply attested
by the famed Sistine Chapel, by its celebrated choir, by his
generous benefactions to the Vatican Library. Nothing
about his personal life suggests evil or corruption. On the
contrary, in view of his personal qualities, apart from a certain naïve lack of prudent judgment, his pontificate promised accomplishment.

But this promise was never fulfilled. Deep involvement in
the intrigues, manoeuvers, schemes of petty Italian politics
tended not only to divert the papacy from the needs of the
universal Church but also to depress its universal character
by transforming it into a temporal princedom. And at the
same time the papal policy of structuring its civil and ecclesiastical administration along family (and national)
lines,[36] tended further to diminish confidence in its sacral
and universal character. "Nepotism became the system of
the Roman states. . . . The nephews were the symbol of
the personal sovereignty of the popes, and at the same time
the props as well as the instruments of their temporal rule,
their trusted ministers and generals."[37]

Sixtus IV, one of five children, was uncle to eleven
nephews and two nieces. "Of the eleven nephews six were
clerics—it was a simple matter to make five of them
cardinals, while the sixth became Bishop of Ferrara and
Patriarch of Antioch. Two of his lay nephews the pope mar-
ried to daughters of the King of Naples, a third to the

[36] Under Callixtus III the Spaniards (Catalans) dominated
Rome, under Pius II the Sienese, under Sixtus IV the Ligurians. The
history of the Colonnas, Orsinis, della Roveres, and Borgias gives
the impression that the Church was peculiarly founded for their
personal benefit.
[37] F. Gregorovius, op. cit., 7, 1, 245.

heiress of the reigning Duke of Urbino, and a fourth to a
daughter of the Duke of Milan. A sixth red hat went to
one of his niece's sons."[38] This neat summary of the nepotism of Sixtus brings out clearly the nature of the sickness
from which the papacy suffered in the late fifteenth century.
It sharply underlines symptoms which spell a fatal prog-
nosis.

Let us review briefly the case of the nephew Piero
Riario,[39] friar, cardinal in his twenty-fifth year, enriched
with a vast income realized from the many sees which he
held simultaneously,[40] ambitious for power, proud, vain
and a lover of luxury "which rendered him utterly unworthy
of the purple." This spendthrift, whose high living astonished even Renaissance Rome,[41] received all from the
Church to which nothing was rendered in return. Worn
out with his riotous life (so typical of the poor man
suddenly become rich), he died in his twenty-eighth year,
"while he gave promise of still better things."

Twenty-one of the twenty-five cardinals[42] who assembled

[38] P. Hughes, A History of the Church 3, 389–90.

[39] He is represented with his brother Girolamo, "one of the worst
men of all this bad time," in Melozzo da Forli's famous fresco. Ibid.,
3, 390.

[40] He held, for example, the important sees of Treviso, Valence,
Mende, Spoleto, Florence, and the benefices of various monastic
foundations. His yearly income was at least a half million dollars, a
staggering private income in that century.

[41] Of Piero Riario it was remarked that his ostentation surpassed
anything that our children will be able to credit, or that our fathers
can remember. Cf. L. Pastor, op. cit., 4, 239.

[42] Sixtus IV had created thirty-four cardinals. Approximately
three-quarters of the cardinals in this conclave owed their dignity to
him. "The serious corruption in the College of Cardinals began
under Sixtus IV. . . ." Cf. ibid., 5, 170; 4, 409.

in the conclave on August 26, 1484—"among the most deplorable in the annals of Church History,"[43]—were Italians. After certain preliminaries, including the preparation of a new Capitulation which would have changed the monarchical constitution of the Church into an aristocratic one[44] (as truly as Conciliarism a generation before would have made it oligarchic), the scrutiny commenced. The first ballot cast seemed to favor the austere Cardinal Marco Barbo, who was well known for his strict morality and earnest desire of reform. The "danger" latent in this candidate did not escape the shrewd notice of Cardinals Giuliano della Rovere and Rodrigo Borgia through whose influence and acute diplomacy the conclave was persuaded to accept the Genoese Giovanni Batista Cibò, Bishop of Molfetta, a most benign non-entity, the father of two illegitimate children (born before he had embraced the clerical state), a man without a will of his own and, therefore, incapable of decision at a time when important decisions had to be made for the good of the Church. He was elected on the morning of August 29, 1484 and took the name Innocent VIII.

In the eight years of his pontificate "nothing of any importance was done . . . for the reform of ecclesiastical abuses."[45] This is not surprising, seeing that Cardinal della

[43] Cf. *ibid.*, 5, 233. But the conclave of 1492, which elected Alexander VI, was equally deplorable.

[44] Obviously the Roman Curia would constitute this new governing aristocracy which more than ever would have the opportunity to 'use' the Church.

[45] Cf. L. Pastor, *op. cit.*, 5, 350. During the pontificate Giovanni de' Medici, second son of Lorenzo, was created cardinal in his fourteenth year!

Rovere to whom Innocent owed so much (both cardinalate and papacy) was his closest confidant and adviser. The cardinal was, as the Florentine Ambassador wrote, "Pope and more than Pope." Where his influence was lacking, it was generously supplied by Cardinal Rodrigo Borgia, already one of the most wealthy and most worldly members of the Curia, the most notorious churchman of his day, and the father of at least four children, Caesar, Juan, Jofré and Lucrezia, who would grow up to plague the Church in the pontificate of their father, the future Alexander VI.

On August 6, 1492—three days after Christopher Columbus had embarked upon his heroic enterprise—the cardinals assembled to elect a successor to Innocent VIII who had died piously on July 25th. Five days later Cardinal Rodrigo Borgia emerged from the conclave as Alexander VI—a man, who in the primitive Church would have been prevented from the lowest of holy orders and compelled to stand at the portal of the church as a public penitent. But in this irresponsible worldly age he proudly ascended the highest pinnacle. With his pontificate the bitter cup of degradation overflows with simony, nepotism, immorality, with every evil of which that gross age was capable. But the indifference and unconcern with which this universal scandal and decay were accepted on all sides, underline the mystery and anguish which run through every page of Church History.

But while others were silent, the voice of the Dominican Friar, Fra Girolamo Savanarola, could be heard vigorously lashing the corruption which he saw on all sides, especially in the Roman Court where moral abuse was notorious.

From the very beginning of his pontificate this voice was a torment to Pope Alexander who used every means at his disposal to silence and banish this prophet of doom who had so completely captured the hearts and minds of all, above all the Florentines. In 1497 Fra Savanarola was excommunicated by Alexander. In the following year he openly declared to the world: "I attest to you in the name of Christ, this Alexander is not a pope. I affirm that he is not a Christian and that he does not even believe in the existence of God." When ordered to cease preaching to the people, he boldly refused. His insolent remark, "The pope cannot order anything contrary to Christian charity or the Gospel," breathes forth a disobedience, revolt, schism,[46] which the Church could not tolerate.

Consumed with a vision of a purified Church, this ardent friar failed as a reformer. Victimized by his holy fanaticism which knew no bounds, and convinced of his prophetic role which exceeded prudence, Fra Savanarola could not inspire that true reform which the Church needed so urgently. His contumacious disobedience proved his undoing. Yet he remains a symbol of the selfless Christian who generously allows himself to be consumed with the hope that a greater good may one day rise from his ashes. On May 25, 1498, his own beloved Florentines brought him to the Piazza della Signoria, hung him by the neck, and

[46] Despite these sharp words, and the even sharper remark: "The Pope is no longer a Christian, he is an infidel, a heretic. As such he has ceased to be Pope," H. Jedin maintains, and rightly so, that "Savanarola was a Thomist and a strict adherent of the doctrine of papal supremacy." H. Jedin, A History of the Council of Trent 1 (St. Louis 1957) 40.

reduced his body to ashes. He died, but it would be long before the last echoes of his pleading agonizing voice died out in the Church which he tried to help.[47]

The pontificate of Alexander VI forms a bridge between the fifteenth and sixteenth centuries. He was elected in 1492 before Columbus had reached the shores of America; at the time of his death, August 18, 1503, he was the first pope to exercise jurisdiction in the New World.[48] His entire adult life, since he was created cardinal in his twenty-fifth year, had been spent in the service of the Church whose destiny he influenced so deeply. Alexander was a patron of art, a politician of skill and an enemy of heresy. He even conceived of a program to reform the Church![49] No pope in the entire history of the papacy has been judged so harshly nor painted in such dark colors as this last Spanish pope. But he was not totally evil. Good things can be told of him.[50] But his greatest failure was the grave irresponsibility which he showed in exposing the Church to corruption and decadence when he had a sacred mandate

[47] "The deep spirituality and the stern asceticism of the Florentine prophet" yielded a rich harvest among the Spanish Dominicans "and thereby prepared the ground for the flowering of the classical Dominican theology of the sixteenth century." Cf. ibid., 1, 142.

[48] One of the noteworthy acts of his pontificate was the division of the New World between Spain and Portugal.

[49] In the sad days after the death of his son in 1497 the pope created a reform-commission of six cardinals to draw up a plan for the thorough renovation of the Church. It never moved beyond the draft stage, and was soon forgotten.

[50] Alexander did take measures to provide for the propagation of the faith in the New World. Some of the first gold discovered there ornaments to this day the vaulting of St. Maria Maggiore.

to protect and guide it as its chief bishop and supreme pastor. "It seemed as though his reign," writes Pastor, "were meant by Providence to demonstrate the truth that though men may hurt the Church they cannot harm her."[51]

One of the tragedies of the sixteenth century is that Francesco Cardinal Piccolomini[52] elected on September 22, 1503 died less than one month later. This austere, devoted churchman, who took the name Pius III in honor of his uncle, promised much good. Pious, studious, sober, and mortified, he was the very antithesis of his predecessor. He answered a real need of the Church. Within three days of his election he informed the Curia in very clear terms that it was his intention to summon a general council for the reformation of the whole Church, the papacy, the Curia, the cardinals and all members down to the lowest. He had the mind and will of a reformer, but not the physical energy or stamina. Death was good to him; for it spared him, now a weak, sick old man, the anguish and toil involved in the completion of his grand scheme. But his death left the Church unreformed.[53]

The pontificates of Julius II (1503–13) and Leo X (1513–21), often characterized as "the age of iron" and

[51] L. Pastor, op. cit., 6, 140.

[52] Even Gregorovius (op. cit., 8, 1, 11) admits that Pius III "was a man of blameless life," though he adds that he "suffered from gout and old age" and was elected "to tide over the crisis" after the death of Alexander VI.

[53] "The second Piccolomini Pope was undoubtedly animated by the best will in the world, but like Marcellus II fifty years later, he died before his plans had taken shape." H. Jedin, op. cit., 1, 75.

"the age of gold," bring to a close the line of pontiffs known
as the popes of the Renaissance. In view of our discussion
of the papacy of the fifteenth century, it scarely seems
necessary to note that the pontificates of these two popes,
one a della Rovere, the other a Medici,[54] form a prolonga-
tion of the spirit of the preceding century, a continuation
of its nepotism, simony, and negligence. The papacy remained fixed in the hands of the same old circle which
used and abused it freely to their own profit. Now we find
a deeper involvement in Italian politics, a stronger preoccupation with the temporal sovereignty of the Papal
States and its independence of the other powers. These
eighteen years bristle with a series of difficult crises of which
the French Church and its commitment to Gallicanism was
the most formidable.

Faced with a schism of the French Church in addition to
the host of perennial problems, Julius II convoked on July
18, 1512 the Fifth Lateran Council.[55] It was conceived as a
very clever, well timed counter-thrust against the attempts
of Louis XII and the schismatical cardinals in league with
him to assemble what surely would have proved the re-
enactment of the antics of the anti-papal council of Pisa
a century before. In the Ninth (May 6, 1514) and Tenth
(May 4, 1515) Sessions of the Council held under Leo X
the question of reform was posed, discussed and "solved."
New laws were enacted, new regulations and measures

[54] Giuliano della Rovere and Giovanni de' Medici.
[55] This Council has been aptly characterized as "the last attempt
at a papal reform of the Church before the break-up of Christian
unity." H. Jedin, op. cit., 1, 128.

against abuses formulated.[56] The whole program, duly promulgated for the good of the Church, went unheeded. And at the risk of seeming cynical, one wonders if the observance of these decrees was seriously intended, for it is questionable whether the heart of this tragic council was committed to reform; and, if reform did not commence in high places, among the Fathers of the Council, it would never reach down to the lowly members of the Church.

Actually it was not law that the Church needed, but observance. The words which Cardinal Contarini addressed to Paul III at a later date are filled with insight into the character of this thoroughly human situation in which ecclesiastical reform is almost always involved: "If Your Holiness wants to bring the Church to a flourishing state, there is no need to make new laws. There is already enough of them. There is need of living books in which one can read the laws, that is to say, cardinals and bishops full of piety and knowledge."[57]

On March 16, 1517, the Lateran Council held its final session. In retrospect the Council appears a dismal failure, for it neither radically changed the *status quo* of the Church nor devised ways and means for her to live and thrive in the new world which was coming into existence. The Fathers of this Council seemed unaware of the fact that the old medieval world having reached the autumn time of her life was slowly but surely dying, and that the Church, largely en-

[56] The very frank, bold, honest memorial, presented to Leo X at this time by the Camaldolese T. Giustiniani and V. Quirini, foreshadows the new spirit of Catholic reform.

[57] L. Pastor, op. cit., 6, 140.

cumbered in its *modus operandi* by medieval survivals, was in need of drastic renovation. One century had passed since the Council of Constance had promulgated its reform program with the hope and promise that the papacy would realize it. During all those long years the word "reform" was on the lips of every Christian seriously interested in the well-being of his Church. It was the dream, the aspiration, the hope of the century. But the pages of the history of this dismal time are filled with the bitterness of unfulfillment. The problems that reform posed did not solve themselves; neglect only begot more neglect; broken promises created general mistrust. The constant appeals to the Holy Spirit, who guides the destinies of the Church, demanded more than good will on the part of its head and members.

In the sixty decisive years from the election of Nicholas V in 1447 until the appearance of Luther's theses is 1517, the fourth year of the pontificate of Leo X, the papacy, without fully realizing it, had become more and more isolated from the concrete realities which surrounded it. The historical sources of the period create the impression of a general incapacity to assess the needs of the Church and an utter powerlessness to provide for them. The history of the whole period is a clear record of growing disaster. So long as the papacy continued to develop in the pattern marked out in the late fifteenth century, it could offer no solace, no hope for universal renewal. The writing on the wall was clear, but it was not read; if it were read, it would not have been fully understood; and, had it been understood, one wonders what measures would or could, have been taken to turn back the overpowering tide which corruption, carelessness, irresponsibility, and abuse had created.

In view of its historical antecedents: the Avignon papacy, the Great Western Schism, the Conciliar movement, and the new humanism under the aegis of the papal court, the Holy See had entered a new climate of thought, a new phase of her existence, a new stage of Western history. The whole trend of fifteenth century history suggests the emergence of a new civilization in which the relations between the papacy and the world would be determined by new values, largely nonreligious and secular. Medieval culture, especially its vigorous intellectual and spiritual ideals, was already withering and evolving into something quite different. The fact that the popes of this time seemed unaware of the vast transition, development, and evolution which was taking place on all levels of human society might be explained by their lack of a sense of history. They were, after all, men whose intellectual lives were formed in the theology and canon law of the day which was far removed from the concreteness of historical *Wissenschaft*, with its stress on genetic growth as a factor in human civilization and culture.

Nowhere in this century is there evidence that the papacy truly estimated the proportions of the disaster which was threatening Christendom; and even where it is clear that this or that devoted churchman had a firm grasp on the significance of the crisis, his criticism was resented, even silenced;[58] or the methods which were employed in the work of reform were invariably incomplete, superficial, halfhearted, unsupported. All reform in the fifteenth century failed in the sense that it was neither universal in extent nor

[58] J. T. Ellis, *Church History and the Seminarian* (St. Meinrad 1961), pp. 14–15.

permanent in character. It was directed more to the correction of particular situations rather than to the general state of the Church. It tended to treat superficial symptoms rather than root causes. It was unorganized, partial, and undisciplined. It depended on a handful of men of good will to accomplish what actually called for the cooperation of the whole collectivity of the Church.

Reform is a dread word, for it imports in some sense revolution, an overturning of invested interests, a cutting away of special privilege, and an abnegation of the personal good in favor of the commonweal. It can have no part with egoism. For the essential *metanoia*—the change of both heart and mind—which is fundamental to reform, demands profound humility. Without the sympathetic, generous cooperation of many individuals reform is impossible; but even more than virtue is required—an intelligent comprehension of the total organism that is to be reformed is also necessary. Without a diagnosis of the malady no remedy can be prescribed; and without the courage to apply the prescription, no cure is likely. True reform must be built on knowledge and courage. But above all it must be *wanted*. It is here that the tragedy of the fifteenth century is most clearly discerned; for in the work of reform—which was on the lips of every churchman—knowledge, courage, and desire were lacking. Reform failed, bcause the very men who were responsible for the well-being of the Church failed in their sacred commitment to her.

The first half of this century was alive with Conciliarism, menacing the monarchical character of the Church; but, at the same time, Conciliarism represented a reform program, one of many attempts to carry out a thorough renovation in the administration of the Church. Its definitive rejection by the Church was a singular victory for the papacy for it preserved the true hierarchical character of the Church. But at this hour of history the papacy should have demonstrated to Christendom how effectively monarchical power could be used for reformation and renovation. Commencing with Nicholas V (1447-1455), the popes dissipated their energies and resources on peripheral issues: the humanism of the Renaissance, the creation of a new Rome, the perennial crusade against Islam, the politics of France, Spain, and Germany, the exhausting struggle between the Colonna and Orsini families, the lavish enrichment of nephews, sons, and whole families of relatives, and all the thousand and one petty problems that marked the history of the fifteenth century City States of Italy.

Many of these issues were of high importance to the full development of Western history, but the involvement of the Church in these matters, often of purely secular interest, distracted her from her true task and weakened her prestige. But more than that, this ill-conceived policy forced the pope into the role of Renaissance prince, a role which considerably diminished the aura of the Church's sacred character which fell ever deeper into shadow. And this unfortunate state of stagnation, however distasteful and unsavory at first, soon became part of everyday life and was taken very much for granted. What most shocks us is not the presence of this or that particular deviation from Christian morality—for surely moral weakness is part of all human history—but rather the cold indifference, the genial tolerance, and the almost callous unconcern with which it was all regarded at the time. It is this form of moral degradation that invaded the highest places in the Church in the last days of that century and prepared the way for the almost universal disaster of the sixteenth century.

A most superficial inspection of the lists of benefices, privileges and preferments which were so liberally bestowed at this time could have foretold with certainty a coming crisis. The malpractices in levying tithes and in collecting annates were notorious. Clerical celibacy was generally neglected, religious life poorly observed, episcopal absenteeism glaring. Some of the most distinguished monasteries in the Western World were held by lay lords *incommendam*; and more than one bishop presided simultaneously over a plurality of sees. Because the episcopacy was poorly chosen, the lower clergy suffered and the laity was deprived of pastoral care. The sacred liturgy, which had long ceased to be a living factor in Christian life, yielded more and more to a popular type piety whose value was questionable. The nominalistic theology of the day, rooted in a worn out scholasticism and out of touch with reality, ceased to influence the minds of men. In fact, it had become the object of scorn and satire. Theology and piety separated with the same finality that faith and reason had foresaken their ancient alliance.

In the midst of all these episodes which rapidly succeeded one another throughout the century, it was clear that northern Europe, especially in the Germanic lands already heavily taxed in support of the Church and the Roman Curia, was becoming restless and resentful, indig-

nant at the humiliations to which it was ruthlessly submitted. Its hostility was sufficiently open to create grave
suspicions in the minds of thoughtful men about the security and the future of the Church in these regions. The serious disorders, religious and political, which John Hus had
created in the kingdom of Bohemia had not vanished with
the flames which had consumed him. In England, the free,
unrestricted exercise of papal power, long resented by the
ruling house of that kingdom, was being gradually diminished by law, and the rebellious spirit of the French Church
is obvious in her audacious claim to the so-called Gallican
liberties. No one in the late fifteenth century save for those
few, very few indeed, who benefited personally from this
universal decay, was satisfied with the alarming state in
which *Christianitas* found herself.

At the beginning of the fifteenth century the criticism of
John Hus was answered with fire. At the end of that same
century, another voice was heard reproaching the Church
for the scandals of both head and members. It was a violent
voice, uncontrolled, direct, frightening rather than persuad-
ing, speaking words which his contemporaries were too callous either to hear or to understand. In 1498 Fra Girolamo
Savanarola died in the flames, like John Hus almost a century before him. His protesting voice against the evil *status
quo* would echo and re-echo throughout the following century. Within twenty-five years, Luther himself by commit-
ing the papal bull to the flames would demonstrate vividly
that violence is of no useful importance in solving serious
problems of the mind and spirit.

On March 16, 1517 the Lateran Council closed. Within

eight months of this event, the Augustinian Friar, Martin Luther had informed the city of Wittenberg of his serious intention of defending ninety-five theses touching on abuses in faith and morals. The pleasure loving, cultivated esthete, Leo X, who was then occupying the throne of St. Peter, scarcely noticed this tiny cloud on the broad horizon of universal Christendom. But before his inept pontificate had terminated, he would be caught up in the first blasts of what would prove to be the greatest storm ever to hit the Church.

V

DIVIDED CHRISTENDOM

At the beginning of the sixteenth century the Church was
suffering acutely from *deformatio*, that consuming disease
which had been growing within it for more than a century
and which would continue to grow until the saving remedy
was applied.[1] As direct offspring of the dying medieval world,
the Church of the early sixteenth century had inherited its
liabilities—abuses, corruption, infamy, weakness, and an
effete administration, as well as the problem of the new
national monarchies.[2] These liabilities, neglected in the
course of the past century, had developed roots of mon-
strous proportions reaching deep down into the very fiber
of the Church and menacing her inner structure. *Deformatio* was a sickness with only *reformatio* could cure. The
discovery and application, therefore, of this healing *reformatio* formed the central problem of the Church of that
day. While Christendom waited for its cure, the sands of

[1] *Deformatio* signifies here a deviation from the norm of perfection, concretely a general state of decadence manifested in widespread abuse, corruption, collapse. Cf. Y. Congar, *Vraie et fausse
réforme dans l'Eglise* (Paris 1950), pp. 356–57.
[2] J. Lortz, *Die Reformation in Deutschland* 1 (Freiburg 1949) 7.

time were running through the hour glass; the cup of
patience, now filled to the brim, was ready to spill over.
The point at which crisis comes to its fullness was at hand,
and the balance was turning on its pivot. The end-phase of
one period of history had been reached. Another was commencing.[3]

On every page of the history of the early fifteen hundreds
one senses the immanence of that crisis within Christendom whose fury was well calculated to bring the Church
close to the brink of universal ruin. Never since 1054, when
Catholic Christendom had tragically divided into East and
West, had the threat of schism been so formidable. Never
before in the Western World had the raison d' être of the
venerable Church of Rome been so profoundly assailed and
so thoroughly questioned as by the Protestant reformers.
The repudiation of the Holy See by a large portion of Europe would form a stunning episode in the history of the
Church. At the opening of the century there had been one
Church in the West. By the middle of the century the
religious unity of Christendom had vanished. At its close
Christianity was splintered into many sects sharply and bitterly opposed in their concept of the Gospel of salvation. It
was the tragic hour in which religious pluralism was born,
the last hour of that united Christendom which the medieval world had created and nurtured. In this period the
seeds of discord gradually grew into an irreparable schism
dividing Christian against Christian into hostile factions.[4]

[3] Cf. R. H. Bainton. *The Reformation of the Sixteenth Century*
(Boston 1952), pp. 23, 51.
[4] The bitterness which the Reformation was to engender is epitomized by Bl. Margaret Clitherow's (d. 1586) words to the minister who wished to pray with her before martyrdom: "I will not pray

Concretely, the religious revolution of the sixteenth century represents the dissolution of the religious unity of the medieval world.

The ultimate explanation of this vast upheaval within the Christian body will ever remain a mystery.[5] It is rooted in a rich complexity of factors political, economical, and social; but it was essentially concerned with religion, with the discovery of the true character of Christianity as the religion of the Gospel of Christ.[6] The undeniably decadent state of the Church in the fifteenth century—especially its moral corruption, progressive secularization, decadent theology, irresponsible administration, and voluntaristic piety—cannot be overlooked as prime factors in bringing down the House of God and dispersing the faithful in that scandalous schism which has not to this day been healed.

The ecclesiastical sources of the period are unanimous in attesting a wide gap between the profession of the saving faith and the honest observance of its salutary precepts by all levels of Christian society. This alarming state of affairs, producing grave tension within the Church also bred impatience, resentment, and rebellion, and, worst of all, the conviction that the historic Church was effete. By all standards the situation was dangerously critical. Its deep significance should not have escaped the notice of the more thoughtful, responsible men of that day. And yet it

---

with you, nor shall you pray with me; neither will I say Amen to your prayers, nor shall you to mine." Cf. M. T. Monro, *Blessed Margaret Clitherow* (New York 1947), p. 101.

[5] J. Lortz, op. cit., 1, 12.

[6] R. H. Bainton, op. cit., p. 3.

is a fact of history that this crisis failed to awaken *within* the Church a true reform of the Church.

Protestantism, as a reform movement, was a revolution of the religious order essentially. It did not arise spontaneously; it was the product of time and circumstance; and, when it acquired a leader and a plan, it burst forth as the proper stimulus was applied. Initiated as early as the beginning of the fifteenth century, it fed on that bitter frustration which the long abuse of religion had created in the heart of the Church, especially in the northern countries of Europe. Smoldering with deep resentment against financial exploitation and ecclesiastical abuse, the German Church discovered in Martin Luther a leader whose theology would be the foundation of reform.[7] The shocking circumstances under which Johann Tetzel preached indulgences stimulated the movement to life.

In view of the dedication of the papacy to the art and architecture of the Renaissance, it is not altogether surprising that in the execution of its grandiose (and expensive) schemes for the embellishment of Rome a blunder should sooner or later be made. The tactical error here was nothing more or less than the plan devised for financing the projected basilica of St. Peter in Rome. With the approval of Leo X a decision was finally reached: a plenary indulgence would be granted to all contributors to the furtherance of this worthy cause, and the preaching of this 'mission of mercy' would be entrusted to a Dominican Friar named Johann Tetzel. The plan received the wholehearted ap-

[7] H. Jedin, A *History of the Council of Trent* 1 (St. Louis 1957) 169: "In attacking indulgences Luther's theory of salvation trenched on a sphere of the Church's life in which undeniable exaggerations and abuses had occurred: theology became reform."

proval and cooperation of Albrecht of Hohenzollern, the most powerful prelate in the German empire, the Archbishop of the venerable see of Mainz, and Bishop of both Magdeburg and Halberstadt—a jurisdiction embracing about one-third of the richest part of Germany. Despite his avarice and blundering this young nobleman, now in his twenty-eighth year, would soon be made a cardinal (March 24, 1518) by Leo X and would come close to being named papal legate of the whole German empire. It was under the auspices of this incompetent ecclesiastic that the indulgence crusade was launched in Germany.

Now it so happened that at the very time that this vast 'apostolic' undertaking was being prepared, Albrecht was in debt to the banking house of Fugger for the sum of approximately 24,000 golden ducats borrowed to pay the Holy See for the various dispensations graciously extended to him to enjoy his lucrative pluralism. Hence, a method was worked out: Friar Tetzel would be allowed to preach the indulgence in all those parts of Germany under Archbishop Albrecht's jurisdiction; the proceeds realized from this enterprise would be neatly divided between pope Leo's project and Fugger. In this way, the basilica would be built, the archbishop would become solvent, and the faithful would have their indulgences.

Apart from the bad theology underlying Tetzel's concept of the application of indulgences to the dead,[8] the whole business was sordid. The fact that a representative of the house of Fugger was allowed to sit side by side with the indulgence preacher, note each financial contribution, and

[8] L. Pastor, op. cit., 7, 349.

estimate the percentage which was due to his employer shows how deeply secularism had eaten its way into the life of the Church. That the Holy See, in the midst of all the proposals and counterproposals for the reform of the Church, especially in light of the grave discontent in Germany and Bohemia, should have allowed its name and prestige to be attached to this abuse, indicates how far it was out of touch with the spirit and need of the time.

At high noon on the Eve of All Saints, October 31, 1517, while the people were gathering in Wittenberg to gain indulgences by honoring the relics of the saints preserved there,[9] Luther posted his ninety-five Latin theses under the title A Disputation on the Power and Efficacy of Indulgences.[10] It was an open invitation to hear theological theses debated publicly "out of love and zeal for the truth and the desire to bring it to light." This dramatic thrust at what appeared to Luther to be a grave misuse of Catholic dogma was conceived as an academic attack on the doctrine of indulgences, especially as Tetzel had conceived it. Thus the twenty-seventh thesis reads: "They preach only human doctrine who say that as soon as the money clinks into the money-chest, the soul flies out of purgatory."[11] But the

[9] P. Hughes, A History of the Church 3, 502: "In the castle church at Wittenberg, which was also the university church, there was preserved one of the most famous of all collections of relics."

[10] Cf. for the text of the theses C. Mirbt, Quellen zur Geschichte des Papsttums und des römischen Katholizismus (4th ed. Leipzig 1924), pp. 253–56. An English translation is to be found in Luther's Works 31: Career of the Reformer 1, ed. J. J. Grimm (Philadelphia 1957) 25–33.

[11] "Homines praedicant, qui statim, ut iactus nummus in cistam tinnierit, evolare dicunt animam."

theses were envisioned as more than a refutation of Tetzel. Motivated by "German national resentment against papal exploitation," Luther was here questioning "the jurisdiction of the pope over purgatory" and the doctrine of the mediatorship of the Church in the work of salvation. He represented indulgences as inducing a wrong state of mind in the Christian.[12]

But the publication of these celebrated theses coincides neither with the birth of the new evangelical theology nor with the egress of Luther from the Church. For as early as 1512, in the well-known Tower episode, he had discovered in the depths of his inner, personal experience the formulation of that saving principle, so very fundamental to his concept of Christianity, that faith alone justifies and the Scripture alone is the norm of faith;[13] and, on the basis of this principle he boldly proceeded to construct his new evangelical theology which represented a thorough reconstruction of the fundamentals of Catholic ecclesiology and soteriology.[14]

In the years between 1517 and 1521 Luther's theses became throughout the length and breadth of the German empire a *cause célèbre* to which no one could afford to remain indifferent. The issues at stake involved the very fiber of Christian civilization. Pope, emperor, bishops, theologians, knights, and peasants were all drawn into the great debate whose last word has not to this day been spoken. Within a short period of time the full import of the new

[12] Cf. R. H. Bainton, *op. cit.*, 40.
[13] H. Jedin, *op. cit.*, 1, 169.
[14] *Ibid.*, 1, 166 ff.

evangelical Christianity manifested itself. In the unfortunate debates at Leipzig (June 27 to July 16, 1519) the astute Dr. Johannes Eck, representing the Catholic cause to which he was enthusiastically devoted, ruthlessly pushed Luther in directions in which he was not prepared to travel. The result of this epoch-making dialogue was to elicit from Luther a public denial of both papal and conciliar infallibility, the supremacy of the Church of Rome in Christendom, and the divine origin of papal authority.[15] Luther had been pushed into new areas of thought, and he would not recoil from the consequences to which the logic of the debate had led him. He hardened in these new ideas which, at first, he never dared even to conceive.

On June 15, 1520 pope Leo X in a solemn bull, *Exsurge Domine*, condemned the Lutheran theses as "errors, heretical, scandalous, false, offensive to pious ears, seductive of simple minds, opposed to the Catholic faith," and threatened their author with excommunication unless he should recant his teaching within a canonically fixed period of time. Far from recanting, Luther showed his determination by publishing in the summer and autumn of 1520 a series of tracts which blistered the papacy while denouncing the whole Catholic sacramental system. Further, on December 10, 1520, he contemptuously consigned to the flames the papal bull, *Exsurge Domine*, a copy of the canon law, Clavio's *Summa* on penance, and other books—all symbols in one way or another of the medieval Church, her legal system

[15] Cf. Luther's *The Leipzig Debate* and his letter (July 20, 1519) to George Spalatin on the debate itself in *Luther's Works* 31, 313–25.

and her way of thought.[16] On January 3, 1521 a second bull
of Pope Leo, *Decet Romanum Pontificem*, put him outside
the pale of the Roman Church. But the desired effect was
not produced, for Luther had gone too far to be intimidated
by papal threats. His bold defiance was a sign that the times
had changed. Luther would not play the role of the martyred John Hus. In fact, viewed in the context of their accomplishment, the two bulls failed dismally, for they received the wholehearted support neither of the German
hierarchy nor of public opinion. The muddle-headed thinking into which Conciliarism had lulled the people, enforced
the conviction "that Luther and his adherents were not definitely cut off from the Church as long as a Council had not
pronounced judgment."[17] At the Diet of Worms in April
1521 he openly defied the emperor and the law of the empire under whose ban he had been placed.[18]

Luther's reform was a revolt against the past one thousand years of history. It rejected the papal and imperial
authority, the teaching office of both pope and council, the

[16] This was the form in which Luther answered Aleander and Eck
who burned his books. It was also an open manifestation of his
hatred for the papacy and Rome. Cf. his pamphlet, "Why the Books
of the Pope and his Disciples were Burned by Doctor Martin
Luther" in *Luther's Works* 31, 385–95.

[17] H. Jedin, *op. cit.*, 1, 177.

[18] The reflection of emperor Charles V, expressed in a letter
(April 19, 1521) written directly after the Diet, is worthy of note.
Thus he writes: "For it is certain that a single friar [Luther] errs in
his opinion which is against all of Christendom and according to
which all of Christianity will be and will always have been in error
both in the past thousand years and even more in the present." Cf.
Luther's Works 32: *Career of the Reformer* 2, ed. G. W. Forell
(Philadelphia 1958) 114, n. 1.

canon law of the Church, the law of the empire, scholastic theology, and traditional Catholic piety. It was not primarily a moral crusade. "Others," said he, "have attacked the life. I attack the doctrine."[19] Not the abuses of Catholicism, but Catholicism itself as an abuse of the Gospel was the object of his onslaught. "I would not have occupied myself with the pope," he wrote after his visit to the Renaissance Rome of Leo X, "if his doctrine had been correct; his evil way of life would not have been a great evil."[20]

Considered in the context of historical Christianity, Luther's reform was in itself a failure because it was directed against the essential structure and system of the Church rather than against that concrete, historical, contingent form which it assumed in his day. Luther's central preoccupation was not with the temporal and transitory aspects of the old Church which cried out for reform and renewal, but with her inner character, doctrine, and authority. The whole tendency and import of his evangelical theology was to negate the past and all its presuppositions. It is a tragedy of no little importance in the history of the Church that this Augustinian friar—one of the most energetic, influential, and courageous reformers of his age—dedicated his life to the destruction of the medieval Church which badly needed reform. His bold rejection of the world in which he was born and educated gives foundation to the view which considers him "a medieval figure ushering in the modern age."

The university circles in which the young Luther was

---

[19] Cf. R. H. Bainton, op. cit., p. 24.
[20] J. Lortz, op. cit., 1, 390.

intellectually bred were heirs to the learning and the mentality of the decadent theology of the so called *via moderna*, characterized by the names of William Ockham, Pierre d'Ailly and Gabriel Biel. It was the intellectual atmosphere born of voluntarism and nominalism, and inclined to divorce faith and reason, theology and piety, morality and religion. With late scholasticism gravitating toward form and method, distinction and terminology, Christian dogma tended to be lost to sight under the façade of theology. This abuse, so profoundly disturbing to the minds of thoughtful men, was to find one of its most effective answers in the Thomistic revival of Thomas de Vio (1469–1534).[21] But even as early as September 1517, Luther had prepared a list of academic theses for a friend which illustrate his resentment against the scholastic method of his day, a resentment which was to color his subsequent polemic.[22] Thus he writes: "Indeed, no one can became a theologian unless he become one without Aristotle. . . . No syllogistic form is valid when applied to divine terms. . . ." And again: "Briefly, the whole Aristotle is to theology as darkness is to light. This in opposition to the scholastics."[23]

But the same resentment against contemporary theology with its unreal approach to religious problems is in evidence

[21] Thomas de Vio, better known as Cajetan, is the author of a commentary on St. Thomas' *Summa* which remains one of the classics of scholasticism. It is not to his discredit that he was not able to dissuade Luther in 1518 from his position, for already the latter's new theology was resting on the presuppposite, *Scriptura sola*.

[22] These theses were prepared by Luther for the disputation of his student Franz Günther. Christopher Scheurl of Nuremberg thought that they would "restore the theology of Christ"!

[23] Cf. *Luther's Works* 31, 9–15.

even among Catholic thinkers who wanted to return both to the Holy Scriptures and to the Fathers of the Church, with the hope of finding there a more spiritual, relevant, and purer understanding of divine revelation. This keenly felt need for return to the primitive sources of Christian doctrine is one of the profound aspirations of the age, one of the earnest hopes of all humanists who were true reformers. Erasmus of Rotterdam (1466–1536) is a clear representative of this school of thought. The following quotation from his *Enchiridion*, written to show the relationship between the scholar and the Christian, is typical:[24]

I find in comparison with the Fathers of the Church our present day theologians are a pathetic group. Most of them lack the elegance, the charm of language, and the style of the Fathers. Content with Aristotle, they treat the mysteries of revelation in the tangled fashion of the logician. . . . It is for this reason that I would recommend that you familiarize yourself with the Fathers. They will lead you to an inner penetration of the spiritual worth it contains. This is certainly to be preferred to the scholastic method that invariably ends up in useless disputation.

Leo X died in Rome on December 1, 1521 without having resolved the Lutheran problem, without in all probability ever having understood its true import. He was succeeded by Cardinal Adrian Dedel of Utrecht who is known in history as Adrian VI.[25] This austere, scholarly, serious-minded Churchman, possessing that rare combination of gifts—learning and sanctity—has the undying credit of be-

[24] Erasmus. *Handbook of the Militant Christian*, tr. J. P. Dolan (Notre Dame 1962), p. 106.

[25] Pope Adrian had been a classmate of Erasmus at Deventer, tutor to the future emperor Charles V, and professor of theology at Louvain. He was the last non-Italian pope.

ing that pope with whom the true reform of the Church awakens. He was realistic, courageous, and practical; and his disposition was such that he was not likely to be side-tracked from his commitment to reform.

At the Diet of Nürnberg on January 3, 1523, the astute papal legate, Francesco Chieregati,[26] read to the astonish-ment of the German princes an *Instructio* drawn up by Pope Adrian himself which not only set forth in clear terms his plans for an honest and thorough reform of the Chuch, but which at the same time forms one of the most remark-able documents in the history of the papacy.[27] For here the pope openly and candidly admitted that from the sins of both clergy and Curia stemmed the present disastrous state of the Church. "The action was without precedent and was never repeated."[28] This celebrated *Instructio* is of sufficient moment in the history of reform to be cited here rather fully:[29]

. . . God has permitted this persecution to be inflicted on His Church because of the sins of men, especially of priests and prelates of the Church. We know that for some years now there have been in this Holy See many abominations, abuses of spiri-tual matters, misuse of authority, and finally all things have be-come decadent. There is no wonder that sickness has passed from the head to the members, from the pontiffs to the lesser prelates. All of us (that is, prelates), and all ecclesiastics have deviated, each in his own way. For a long time there have been none who have done good, not even one. . . . Wherefore, in what

[26] Chieregati had been sent to Nürnberg to see to it that the pro-visions of the bull, *Exsurge Domine*, and the Diet of Worms were implemented.
[27] L. Pastor, op. cit., 9, 132.
[28] H. Jedin, op. cit., 1, 210.
[29] C. Mirbt, op. cit., p. 261.

touches on Our office, We promise you that We will use all means, that this Curia first of all, whence perhaps all this evil has issued, shall be so reformed, that just as corruption has passed from here unto all the lesser parts of the Church, so from here the health and reformation of all will proceed. Let no one be astonished, if he should note that not all abuses and errors are immediately corrected by Us. The sickness is indeed inveterate. It is not a simple illness, but a complicated and multiple one. Its cure must proceed step by step, and first we must handle the more grave and dangerous ills lest in our eagerness that everything be reformed at once, we wreck the whole work. . . .

Despite "the broad-minded candour" of the *Instructio* with its good will, honesty, and courage in openly defining and describing the sickness which afflicted the body of Christendom, even humbly tracing its roots to the highest places in the Church, it "fell flat." "Reforms had been promised too often and never implemented, so no one believed him."[30] And the Reformers far from seeing in this important document evidence that the papacy, once again conscious of its high dignity, had indeed commenced in all earnestness the long-waited reform, reviled the pope with deplorable abuse. "Luther did not think it worth his trouble even to take notice of Adrian's good intentions. He saw in him only the Anti-Christ" . . . the mouthpiece of Satan and his special minister.[31] Nor was this frank document favorably received by the Curia who saw in it nothing more than an advantage to Lutheran polemic against the Church.[32]

[30] H. Jedin, *op. cit.*, 1, 211.
[31] L. Pastor, *op. cit.*, 9, 142.
[32] This mentality ("What will the Protestants say?") will, to the great detriment of Catholic freedom, master the life and thought of the Church for centuries.

On September 14, 1523, Adrian VI died, a victim to the heavy burden of his pontifical office which he faithfully executed and to the scathing odium to which the Italians cruelly subjected him.[33] In the course of a pontificate that lasted not much more than a year, he had brought new life and dignity to the papacy, ravaged now for more than a century. His objectivity of mind and his clarity of vision, joined to outstanding selflessness and courage, made him an ideal reform pope. And though his actual accomplishments never equalled his high aspirations and designs, the reform spirit which he had engendered and nurtured, was to come to full flowering in the Council of Trent (1545–63). Adrian's work had not been in vain.[34]

But his successor, the Medici pope Clement VII (1523–34) was scarcely suited by disposition and temperament to implement the reform which he had formulated in such striking terms. Lacking courage and determination, pope Clement despite his personal integrity was a man of indecision. He evaded rather than solved problems; and a host of unsolved problems plagued his pontificate. In view of the fact that his age was filled with the problems which demanded realistic solutions, his reign was tragic.[35] It wit-

[33] Even in death "the dead man was assailed as an ass, wolf and harpy, and compared to Caracalla and Nero; Pasquino's statue was decorated with ribald verses." Cf. L. Pastor, op. cit., 9, 222. Why? Because he was not an Italian, therefore a *barbarian*, and because he was a reformer, therefore a *tyrant*. The mentality in question does not speak well for the 'broad-minded' Italian humanists of that time.

[34] Cf. the glowing tribute of pope Adrian in L. Pastor, op. cit., 9, 229.

[35] He has been described as "perhaps the most unfortunate of all the popes who have ever occupied the Roman See." Cf. F. X. Seppelt, *Geschichte der Päpste* 4 (Munich 1957) 452.

nessed the beginnings of the dissolution of the venerable Church in England, as it became clearer and clearer that the scandalous divorce proceedings of Henry VIII would surely come to naught; it also witnessed the most terrifying, humiliating disaster which the city of Rome had experienced since the furious Gothic invasions a thousand years before.[36] Both of these lamentable tragedies stemmed from two selfwilled Christian monarchs, emperor Charles V and king Henry VIII. Yet neither of these two principals had been shrewdly assessed by those curial officials whose business it was to evaluate the leading personalities of the day. On the contrary, it seems that both had been underestimated. The potentialities of the two monarchs for striking back had been dangerously minimized. In each case papal policy based on delaying tactics, was ill calculated; and the result was formidable for the Church of Rome which the army of Charles V scourged and from which the kingdom of Henry VIII separated.

When Clement VII died in 1534, the Reformation as a religious movement had reached formidable proportions. It had spread widely throughout the German empire and had invaded France through John Calvin. With the opening of the schism of Henry VIII nine hundred years of history were negated. The universal Church, still unreformed, was

[36] Cf. on the *Sacco di Roma* L. Pastor, *op. cit.*, 9, 388–423. While it cannot be maintained that Charles directly willed the sack of Rome, he is not altogether without blame. "He certainly had wished to punish the Pope and to render his enmity innocuous . . . He had also expressed himself so ambiguously that it might well be supposed that he would see without displeasure his troops requiting themselves with the plunder of Rome . . ." Cf. L. Pastor, *op. cit.*, 9, 444–45.

now divided. Men had not become better but alienated
from one another. The Council, the longed-for panacea,
was still a dream of the future. Remedies had indeed been
applied to the ills from which the Church had been suffering; but it was already clear that the old ways and means
were powerless. The law of the empire against heresy was
ineffectual and papal bulls went unheeded. It was no longer
possible to burn dissenters and for all practical purposes the
Inquisition, as a legal instrument, was dead. It was clearly a
question of finding a new approach to the problem of renovation and reform.

In 1534 the crisis in Christendom had become so intricate and acute that it must have seemed that only a pope,
who would be at once both saint and genius could resolve
it. Although the Church received the services of neither
saint nor genius, in Paul III (1534–49), Alessandro Farnese,
it found a man of strength, intelligence, and decision. Here
was a pope who had the vision to see that the work of reform must be the common work of the Church itself, that,
while inspired by wise and experienced administration, it
must essentially be a common project. With Paul III the
sun of a new age in the history of the Church began to
dawn and the hopes of the Catholic world to arise from
darkness. The highwater mark of the flood had been
reached and with him the waters of destruction began to
recede.

From the pontificate of this intrepid pope there has come
down to us a document, closely related in spirit and tone to
the *Instructio* of Pope Adrian VI. It represents the work of
nine prelates (curial canonists excluded) who were commis-

sioned by Paul III to prepare a candid critique of the general state of the Church, the papacy, and the Roman Curia. The deliberations, conducted with papal approval in an atmosphere of the utmost freedom, lasted from November 1536 until February 1537. Their conclusions are epitomized in the famous *Consilium de emendanda Ecclesia*[37] which commences:

Most Holy Father, we are quite unable to express how grateful the Christian commonwealth ought to be to the good and great God for setting you in these days over His flock and giving you such a spirit. Indeed, we cannot hope even to understand what gratitude it owes to Him. For the Spirit of God, who, as the prophet says, has shored up the very powers of heaven, has decreed to restore through you the Church of Christ that is now collapsing and indeed almost in ruins, to put a supporting hand to the tottering structure, to raise it to its former nobility and give it back its former beauty. Of this divine intention we are sure—we whom Your Holiness has summoned, whom You have bidden make known to You, without respect for any man or for Your own or anyone else's interest, those abuses, those serious ills, from which the Church of God and especially this Roman Curia has long been suffering. These deadly ills have little by little grown ever more serious and have led to the great shambles that now confront us. Your Holiness knows well the source of these evils: some of the pontiffs who preceded You had "itching ears," as the Apostle Paul puts it, and "heaped up to themselves teachers according to their lusts," not to learn from them what their duty was but to find by their skill and cleverness the justification for their own pleasure. The result of this course was to be expected. At all times flattery follows power like a shadow, and truth is always hard-put to reach the ear of princes. But now teachers come forward to proclaim that the Pope is the master of all benefices and, since the master may sell his own property, the pope may not be accused of simony. In like fashion they taught that the pope's wish, whatever its quality, is the norm for

[37] Cf. C. Mirbt, *op. cit.*, p. 267.

his enterprises and actions. The consequence? Whatever he please, he may do. From this source, as from the Trojan horse of old, these many abuses and serious ills have burst forth upon the Church of God. Under them she has struggled, as we see, almost unto despair of her salvation. Report of this situation has reached even to the infidel (please, Your Holiness, believe those who know), and it is the prime reason why he derides the Christian religion. Thus because of us—because of *us!*—the name of Christ is blasphemed among the Gentiles.

Then the document proceeds to outline in detail the various areas of ecclesiastical life which most pressingly require a renovation.

The highly critical approach of the commission, its skilled insight into the Curial administration as a source of abuse, its candor, honesty and objectivity in recommending revision and change in ecclesiastical life, made it a suitable instrument for devising a realistic reform program. The commission primarily aimed at the renewal of the pastoral ministry in the Church, a perennial source of abuse and scandal, but it also directed its attention to the highest administrative level in the Church. "With unheard of boldness," writes Jedin, "the document opened the offensive for the reform movement with a blow against the citadel of the Roman Curia on the conquest of which hung the fate of the Church."[38] In the debate on the *Consilium* which took place before the pope on March 9, 1537 the reform program did not go unchallenged. Cardinal Guidiccioni argued that the reform plan was vitiated by its unrealistic approach to ecclesiastical problems by its naïve advocacy of return to the primitive Christian spirit, by its unwarranted attack on the Curia, and by its revolutionary character. Cardinal

[38] H. Jedin, *op. cit.*, 1, 426.

Nicholas von Schönberg argued that the document in its realistic attack on the Curia and the papacy offered consolation and support to the Lutheran position.

But the new churchmen, who began to appear in Roman circles at this time, refused to accept the old curial approach; they believed that self-criticism could be salutary and exemplary. The new mentality is delineated clearly in the remark of Cardinal Contarini to the Pope, made by way of refutation to the opponents of the reform program:[39]

Rest assured that nothing will disarm the calumnies of the Lutherans and intimidate the King of England more effectively than a reform of the Curia and the clergy. The attempt to justify all the actions of the popes would be arduous and in fact an endless undertaking. We cast no stones at your predecessors, but from you the world expects better things.

The subsequent history of the Church would prove that Contarini was basically correct but not before it had proved that he had greatly overestimated the good will of the German Reformers.

The *Consilium* was essentially a confidential document. As part of the secret business of the Holy See its contents were to be restricted to a small circle of administrators and experts whose candid advice had been asked by Paul III. It was in no sense a public report, but through a bad breach of confidence it soon fell into dishonest hands, was published early in 1538 and was shortly distributed throughout Europe. The Lutherans made capital of it, seeing here a confirmation of all the defamations which they had heaped upon the papacy in the past years. Luther himself translated it into German with a most scandalous, irresponsible, and

[39] *Ibid.*, p. 431.

inflammatory attack on its authors, especially on Pope Paul. "In all this there was not the slightest understanding that a genuine spirit of reform was active in Rome." It was also a sign that, since the *Instructio* of Pope Adrian in 1523, the Reformers had not drawn closer to the reforming spirit of the old Church.[40]

As we have seen above, the fifteenth-century Church had pinned its hopes of reform on the ecumenical councils. Despite its failure to instigate reformation, the idea persisted that reform would ultimately be realized by a general council. From a very early date in his public career Luther had appealed to an ecumenical council as the sole tribunal in Christendom from which he could expect justice. But in the twenty-five years (1517–42) since his first appeal to a council, the conciliar theology of the Protestants had developed in directions widely different from the traditional Catholic thinking. By 1542 it was unthinkable that Protestants (with few exceptions) and Catholics could sit down together at an ecumenical council, summoned and presided over by the pope. Agreement on the character and meaning of an ecumenical council was no longer in evidence. It was inconceivable that its decisions would be accepted unanimously.[41] But still the Catholic world had high hopes that it would find in an ecumenical council *the* instrument for reform and renewal of the Church in head and members. This was certainly the hope of the divided German Church;

[40] In this regard, Vatican Council II is a milestone.
[41] Cf. on the Protestant concept of the ecumenical council M. Seils, "Das ökumenische Konzil in der lutherischen Theologie," and J. L. Leuba, "Das ökumenische Konzil in der reformierten Theologie," in *Die ökumenischen Konzile der Christenheit* (Stuttgart 1961), pp. 333–72, 373–92.

and it was to the realization of this hope that Pope Paul turned his attention early in his pontificate.

In the space of this short essay it is not possible to trace the various contradictory lines of thought that Paul III had to reconcile nor the enormous obstacles which he had to mount, before a council could be summoned. The movement of Church History in the first half of the sixteenth century had created a vast network of conflicting forces and interests which had to be properly managed: the antagonism between Charles V and Francis I, the German mistrust of Italy and the Roman Curia, the survivals of Conciliarism, the egoism of Gallicanism, the scandalous breach between Catholic and Protestants in the Germanic lands, and the ever present pressure of vested interests on all levels of ecclesiastical life. Every aspect of the long proceedings leading up to the convocation of the council of Trent was filled with threat and challenge; and its preparation, almost up to the opening session, is marked with failure and disappointment.[42]

In Paul III the Church had found a pope possessed of the necessary determination, will power and energy to overcome all difficulties, to remove every obstacle, and to resolve every doubt. On May 22, 1542 he issued the bull of convocation. An ecumenical council would meet at Trent

to one end, to ponder, discuss, execute and bring speedily and happily to the desired result whatever things pertain to the purity and truth of the Christian religion, to the restoration of what is good and the correction of bad morals, to the peace,

[42] A summary of the difficult events leading up to the Council of Trent is presented by P. Hughes, *The Church in Crisis* (New York 1961), pp. 301–32.

unity and harmony of Christians among themselves, of the princes as well as of the people, and whatever is necessary to repulse those attacks of barbarians and infidels whereby they seek the overthrow of all Christendom.[43]

On December 13, 1545 the nineteenth ecumenical council solemnly opened at Trent under the presidency of the papal legates, Cardinals del Monte, Cervini, and Pole.

The spirit which animated the Council of Trent at the time of its inception is vividly expressed in an address which Cardinal Pole prepared for the second public session of the Council on January 7, 1546. His frank evaluation of the desperate state of the Church, and his accurate diagnosis of the causes which had lead to this alarming situation were to be normative for the subsequent reform work of the Council. In one of the most stirring pieces of oratory heard throughout the eighteen years of public sessions, the Cardinal reminded his brother bishops of their personal responsibility for the grave ecclesiastical evils which they had assembled to correct:[44]

But if we are to speak the truth we cannot do otherwise than confess that we are conscious of having been greatly wanting in fulfilling the duties imposed on us; and indeed of having in no small part been the cause of the very evils we have been summoned to mend. . . . Before the tribunal of God's mercy we, the shepherds, should make ourselves responsible for all the evils now burdening the flock of Christ. The sins of all we should take upon ourselves, not in generosity but in justice; because the truth is that of all these evils we are in great part the cause, and

[43] Cf. H. J. Schroeder, *Canons and Decrees of the Council of Trent* (St. Louis 1941), p. 9.

[44] Actually the Cardinal's address was read by Angelus Mascarelli, the Secretary of the Council. It is translated by V. McNabb, "Cardinal Pole's Eirenikon," *Dublin Review* 198 (1936) 149–60.

therefore we should implore the divine mercy through Jesus Christ. If any should think that in calling ourselves, who are the shepherds, a cause of the evils burdening the Church, we are using undue bitterness and exaggeration of speech, rather than the truth, facts themselves which cannot lie will bear us witness. Let us therefore scan for a moment the evils burdening the Church and, at the same time, our own sins. . . .

The author of these words, which form a triptych with the *Instructio* and the *Consilium de emendanda ecclesia*, was well qualified to speak. As victim of the hatred of his kinsman, Henry VIII, and the son of the martyred Catholic Countess of Salisbury, he had personally witnessed the fearful destruction of the ancient faith in his native England. He knew by experience the harsh realities of the Reformation. His approach to reform therefore was realistic, candid and serious.

Within a matter of weeks after Cardinal Pole's *Eirenikon*, Martin Luther died (Feb. 18, 1546). The general council to which he had appealed more than once was finally in session, but without his sharing in its reform, the work to which he had dedicated his life. Already the evangelical church had established itself as a distinct part of Christianity. The old religious unity of Christendom was splintered. Pluralism had invaded a large part of the Western World. The Council of Trent, convoked twenty-eight years after the appearance of Luther's theses, was powerless to change all that, but it could gather together the fragments, restore, renew and rejuvenate the Church, and prepare her for hundreds of years more of life.

The Council of Trent lasted almost eighteen years (Dec. 13, 1545 to Dec. 4, 1563) and held twenty-five solemn ses-

sions in addition to countless private ones. It suffered two
suspensions (1547–51 and 1552–62). It was first convoked
to Mantua, then to Vicenza, convened at Trent, transferred
to Bologna, and later returned to Trent where its last session was held. It was convoked by Paul III, survived the
pontificates of Julius III and Paul IV, closed under Pius IV;
it outlived the great Holy Roman Emperor Charles V, King
Francis I of France, and Henry VIII of England. Its last
session was held almost a half century after the first beginning of the Lutheran controversy, and at the time of its
closure the world had substantially changed.

As an aspect of the Catholic Counter-Reformation or the
Catholic Reform, the Council of Trent was deeply concerned with the correction of moral abuse; but it would be
far from the truth to imagine that moral reform was its only
purpose. In the eyes of Paul III Protestantism represented
something far more than a crusade for morality. Its new
theology negated the doctrinal foundation of the Church's
hierarchical and sacerdotal (sacrifice and sacraments) system and this negation created a problem that could not be
neglected. When Martin Luther in the Leipzig Debate attacked the papacy as a mere human creation, a doctrinal
deviation from primitive Christianity, his reformation became in Catholic eyes a serious deformation. Cardinal Cajetan and Dr. Eck at an early date regarded his schism as a
heresy. Accordingly, Paul III wanted the Fathers of the
Council to handle dogmatic questions before disciplinary
measures, or at least consider the two, dogma and discipline
simultaneously. Working in this direction, therefore, the
Council showed that it had properly grasped the character

of the difficult problem of faith and morals which had to be solved.

The dogmatic decrees which Trent formulated without ever mentioning the names of Luther, Calvin, Zwingli or the other reformers, so defined the Catholic faith "that the purity of the Gospel may be preserved in the Church after the errors have been removed." Almost all the articles of the faith (Scripture, tradition, original sin, justification, the sacraments, the Mass, purgatory and indulgences) which the Protestant reformers had attacked or negated, were reviewed and re-expressed in clearer terms. The language in which the Fathers formulated their decrees, was at first biblical and patristic, later in the Council more scholastic and technical; its aim was to be irenic and pastoral, though the polemic spirit of the time caused it to be apologetic and, at times, even contentious. It defined Catholic dogma but it never intended that its definitions be definitive in the sense that all future discussion, interpretation and development be precluded. In terms of the external pressures under which the Fathers of Trent worked, their contribution represents an important stage in the history of theology.

The Tridentine reform decrees touch all grades in the Church, bishops, priests, clerics, religious, and the laity. The Church is to be renewed by renewing her members, especially the episcopacy which is exhorted to provide for the Church a clergy, competently educated and religiously formed. Concretely the Council envisioned a reform of the apostolic ministry of the Church by providing a clergy educated to preach and teach the Word of God. It is of no small significance that the first reform decree (Fifth session, June 17, 1546) provides for the establishment of lecture-

ships in Holy Scripture and the liberal arts (as a propae-
deutic for biblical studies), and decrees that the bishops
"are bound personally . . . to preach the Gospel of Jesus
Christ." Looked at *in toto*, the reform decrees are ordered
to the creation in the Church of an atmosphere of holiness
in which the work of Christ might prosper.

But in one important matter the Council of Trent failed.
It did no reconcile the Protestants nor did it heal the breach
in Christendom. Though the German Evangelicals had
been invited to all three periods of the sessions of Trent
"that they may and shall enjoy full liberty to confer, make
proposals and discuss those things that are to be discussed
in the council; to come freely and safely to the ecumenical
council, to remain and sojourn there and to propose there-
in, in writing as well as orally, as many articles as may seem
good to them, to deliberate with the Fathers . . . and without any abuse and contumely dispute with them . . . and
depart whenever they please."[45] But a successful rapproche-
ment was never concluded. After the council it was too late.
Positions had been taken. Decisions had been made. Nothing would be relinquished. Nothing would be changed. The
Protestants would not accept the decrees of Trent, and the
Catholics could not relinquish them. The extent to which
the Council of Trent forms an obstacle to cherished reunion remains problematic to this day.[46]

[45] Session 18, Feb. 26, 1562. Cf. H. J. Schroeder, *op. cit.*, p. 127.
[46] Cf. H. Jedin, "Ist das Konzil von Trient ein Hindernis der
Wiedervereinigung?" *Ephemerides theologicae Lovanienses* 38
(1962) 841–55. Cf. also M. Lackmann, *The Augsburg Confession
and Catholic Unity* (New York 1963), p. 26: ". . . the Catholic
task of the Reformation period cannot be regarded as finished—
neither was it finished by the Council of Trent."

Divided Christendom—the Western World split into two great segments, the Catholic and the Protestant, both believing in Christ and at the same time repudiating one another—is the extraordinary legacy which the pre-Reformation Church has willed to us. At some undefined point of future time, when religious unity has been once again achieved and the old schism definitively healed, this epoch of history will prove a scandal in the annals of the Church whose founder said, "I pray . . . that all may be one, even as Thou, Father, in Me and I in Thee; that they also may be one in us, that the world may believe that Thou hast sent me." The purpose of this essay is not to fix blame but rather, in understanding more and more of the human side of the Church and her human weakness, to be able to provide for her in all seasons. The collapse of Western Christendom, which commenced in the late thirteenth century and terminated two centuries later, was rooted in human error and human failing. It is ever the task of the Christian in pondering the past history of his Church to grasp the significance of the present and to provide for the future.

VI

CONCLUSION: THE REFORM
OF THE CHURCH

In the pages of this essay we have been discussing in very broad outline the Church in relation to reform in one period of her long history, the centuries before the Reformation. But the dark picture of ecclesiastical life in these years does not represent the whole state of affairs. The Church was indeed sick. Almost everyone recognized that at the time. But the sickness was not unto death. She had sufficient vital resources to produce the giants, both saints and scholars, of the Counter-Reformation; and the grave abuses and scandals on all levels of ecclesiastical life—so clearly symptomatic of that internal malady from which the Church was then suffering—were finally corrected by pope and council. The Church was indeed reformed because hidden deep within her was the power of rejuvenation through the abiding presence of the Holy Spirit.

If the theological and biblical learning of that time was generally stagnant, the Church was not totally deprived of first-rate scholars. Christian humanism was more than a match for the pagan humanism of the time. And the popes

of the Renaissance, while not qualifying as distinguished
spiritual leaders, succeeded in enriching the Western
World with great art, literature, and architecture—a heritage that no student of culture can overlook. The sixteenth
century witnessed the brilliant creation of new forms of religious life and thought which considerably enriched the
Church. But most important of all, this century demonstrated with crystal clarity that there were still Catholics
prepared to give their lives as testimonials to the old faith.

Throughout history the Church is never *all* this way or
that way. As City of God, the Church on earth is made up
of both the good and the bad. But in the century before the
Reformation as the balance tipped dangerously low, the
reform of the Church in head and members posed a problem that through gross neglect grew into a formidable crisis;
and, this crisis stubbornly persisted until the reform of
the highest levels of the Church had seeped far down into
the lowest classes of Christendom. With the coming of
Adrian VI (d. 1523) and Paul III (d. 1549), whose pontificates paved the way for the Catholic Reformation, the total
complexion of the papacy began to change in a direction
which has not since been essentially altered; and the sweep-
ing reform-decrees of the Council of Trent brought about
important changes within the Church which truly renewed
without destroying her. The gigantic achievements of the
Catholic Churchmen of the late sixteenth and early seven-
teenth centuries are a living reminder that the Divine Assistance is always with the Church.

It would be far from the truth to describe the contemporary Church as facing a situation which parallels the

crisis of the late Middle Ages. The current problem is neither moral nor doctrinal reform; it is much more concerned with bringing our doctrinal and moral teaching to bear on the world in which we live. The central question here is the cultural adjustment of the Church to the new civilization which is being born, and her effective integration into contemporary life. The task of the Church is never one of mere survival in the world. Even in the age of the martyrs, in the very depths of the catacombs, the Church, far from assuming the role of one fighting for survival, began in all earnestness to create her own art and architecture, her theology, law, and liturgy; and, in the years after the 'Edict' of toleration (313) by vital participation in the affairs of men she succeeded in helping to create a new culture and civilization. The Church because of her unique relation to both God and man can perform this service again and again, if she has the cooperation of men courageous, intelligent, and patient.

In her quest for a new culture the Church must be ready to relinquish the old. This does not mean the destruction or annihilation of a past heritage, but rather its reinterpretation and transformation into new modes of expression. And in this vast work, which moves slowly through time, the Church must make use of the best features of modern culture. The world is at her service, in fact eager, far more than we suspect, to help in this work. In return she awaits inspiration, understanding, and encouragement. The Church must once again become to the world a symbol not merely of doctrine but also of beauty. Of old the Church has performed this task for human society. Once she was

affiliated with the culture of Late Antiquity, later with the
new medieval culture, still later with the culture of the
Renaissance, the Baroque and Classicism. A most casual
visit to any museum will prove the variety and richness of
Catholic influence on Western esthetics.

All through history the Church has shown an intense
interest in beauty and truth. She has not only allowed, but
actually fostered cultural development in widely different
directions; and, in other areas, for example theology and
spirituality, she has always admitted the greatest range of
diversity compatible with her understanding of the Gospel.
When the Church's method of self-expression becomes an-
tiquated and deformed, reform becames imperative. Because
both the Church and her culture are living, there must be
room for growth and development. The Church is not a
museum but a living community. Hence the forms and
modes of Catholic life change and must change in accord
with the law of life. No amount of pressure or suppression
can prevent development, flux, motion. Death is motion-
less. Life is active.

Permanence in the midst of change is characteristic of
the Church. But permanence pertains to her essential being,
to the very substance of her soul, to the things which she
has received from Christ as part of her essential character.
Change refers to progress, to the contingents which she has
acquired in the course of history, to the accidentals which
come from man. It is in this area of ecclesiastical life that
renewal is imperative. While the Church owes it to Christ
to preserve her identity in the ebb and flow of history, still
she owes it to herself to remove survivals of a past age, those
antique modes and methods which the modern world

neither understands nor respects. She must never allow her universal, almost timeless, mission to be absorbed by the particular, the egotistical, the contingent.

Our age has this in common with the age of Trent, that one great phase of history and culture is terminating, another is being born. The old is passing, the new emerging, and no one can retard this motion. The Church as an institution in this world cannot stand apart from this genetic process. It too must grow and develop parallel to the world about it. The realism, honesty, humility, and concern which we find in the *Instructio* of Adrian VI, the *Consilium de emandanda ecclesia* of Paul III, and the *Eirenikon* of Cardinal Pole helped to create an atmosphere for renewal of the Church. In fact, it was the critical spirit of these documents that transformed the disturbed Church of the dying Middle Ages into the energetic, resourceful Church of the Counter-Reformation. These documents are not face-saving devices, instruments of officialdom, legal formalities. They propose neither to solve problems by slogan nor to allow problems to solve themselves. They represent rather the work of shrewd men, who thoroughly appreciated the value of self-criticism and self-evaluation as the essential presuppositions of true reform and true progress. These men did not fear to ask questions nor to hear their answers. What they heard may have saddened them deeply, but it did not frighten or crush them. They faced evidence and let it speak for itself. They neither took refuge in their official prerogatives nor were personally offended by frank criticism of the episcopal body to which they belonged. Finally, they were skilled Churchmen who, in distinguishing between the sacred character of their office and the human personality which occupied it, were enabled to rise above the particular good of the individual to the universal good of the Church.

As the Tridentine churchmen assisted the Church in her passage from the Middle Ages to the Modern World, so it is our task to assist the same Church in her passage from the Modern World to that new age which has not yet been named. We must facilitate her organic development, put new ways and means at her disposal, bring to her service the fullness of our human talents, make her mobile by pruning away the nonessential commitments of the past ages. Obviously this delicate task requires men of sanctity, intelligence, judgment, and courage. Precisely because the Church is the Mystical Body of Christ, its reform and renovation must always rest in the hands of holy men who appreciate the sacred character of their reforming office.

History has shown repeatedly, however, that sanctity alone, apart from other qualities, is not sufficient for solving the difficult problems which ecclesiastical reform poses. Intelligence, learning, and wisdom are also required. The true reformer must understand the Church (and value it) deeply, as deeply as its inner mystery allows. While aware of her supernatural and mystical character he may not neglect her human and historical aspects, those areas in which she is most vulnerable. The Church is more than a theological concept. She is a concrete, living organism sharing in history through her human members who are weak and defectible; in consequence, she is in perennial need of a corporate examination of conscience, of honest self-evaluation, of that self-criticism without which there can be no true reform.

But every serious, prudent reform-critique must ultimately be based on an objective comparison of the Church, as she is in history, with the Church as she should be by design. The less significant the deviation between the two, the less need of reform. Apart from this criticism, it is difficult to discover the good and the bad, the relevant and the insignificant, the necessary and the contingent; and apart from this critical appraisal it is almost impossible to discover ways and means of leading the Church upward and onward to new achievement. "As a Church of men, sinful men," writes Hans Küng, "the Church though of divine foundation needs criticizing, as the Church of God she is, more than any other institution, worth criticizing."

But if criticism is essential to the growth and the development of the Church, to her preservation from decline and decadence in all areas, caution and prudence are the necessary qualifications of the one who exercises this function. In the modern age mass communications reach down to every level of society, and society is no longer Christian. To avoid public scandal and personal offense, therefore, the criticism which we offer should be dignified, controlled, responsible, reasonable, and submissive. It should be timely, for "every thing and every act . . . has its kairos, its 'due time' "; and, it should be selective, for certain areas of their very nature are outside of critical consideration. Obviously there is no place for the slanderous, the sensational, and the rebellious, for criticism is a work of charity looking to the never ending reform and renewal of the Church as she moves through human history.

In the century before the Reformation, criticism was to

be heard on all sides. Much of it was anti-religious, but a certain portion of it, which was of high caliber, went unheeded. The price that was paid for this administrative irresponsibility was very high indeed; it is, in fact, a debt which has not yet been fully liquidated and which should be a reminder that history punishes severely. In completing the work which Christ gave to her, the Church is not assured of a continued divine revelation instructing her at each decisive moment of her existence; nor does she have the right to expect a chain of miracles to rescue her from every crisis into which history plunges her. Truly she has always with her the Divine Assistance, but this special providence of God does not negate the cooperative efforts of her human members. The Mystical Body represents all classes of men—the soldier, the cleric, the merchant, the statesman—but also those special men whose deep knowledge of things human and divine fits them in a peculiar way to throw light on the problems and crises which the Church must solve, frequently at the peril of her life. These talented men should be assured a most full and free opportunity to serve their Church with those rare gifts of intelligence and understanding with which God has blessed them.

The Church belongs to no individual nor collectivity. Through Christ it is God's. Those to whom the official care of souls is entrusted, exercise a most sacred trust. Their responsibility is peculiarly difficult, since ecclesiastical administrators are neither totally omniscient nor universally infallible. They must administer the Church, not as a private possession, but as the Kingdom of God. Cut off from the trends of contemporary thought and of current problems, they can be readily victimized by egoism. "At all times," reads the *Consilium de emendanda ecclesia*, "flattery follows like a shadow, and truth is hard put to reach the ears of princes." The warning here is salutary to all. Only a largeness of spirit, an openness of mind, a readiness to hear the pros and cons of an issue, and a willingness to listen to criticism constitute an effective antidote to that self-centered kind of government which almost invariably brings the Church to the brink of disaster.

In the *Eirenikon* of Cardinal Pole, cited above, there are lines which give a significant viewpoint of the problem of criticism and reform in the Church. "All the more willingly shall we fulfill this duty of exhortation or of warning because when we exhort you to do what befits so great a gathering or on the contrary warn you, we are exhorting or warning ourselves, who are in the same bark with you, and are exposed with you to the same dangers and the same storm." These words re-echo the solemn moment in the ancient rite of Ordination when the bishop enthroned before his people turns and asks their help in deciding the personal worthiness of the deacons whom he is about to raise to the priesthood:

My dear brothers, just as the captain of a ship and those who travel with him alike have reason on their journey either to feel secure or else imperiled, so too must all who have a common interest be of the same mind. Not without reason, then, did our Fathers establish the custom that the people be consulted about the choice of those who are to be raised to the ministry of the altar. For at times the minority knows things about the life and character of a candidate which is not known by the majority. And it follows that the people will be more ready to render obedience to a priest, if they have been permitted a voice in approving him for Holy Orders. . . . It is my opinion that these candidates are deserving of promotion to a higher honor in the ranks of the Church. But still the advice of many people must be sought, for if only one or a few be allowed to voice their approval, there would be danger of an assent biased by friendship or family ties . . .

These venerable words voice the salutary persuasion that the commonweal of the whole Church, its prosperity and its adversity, is rooted in the people of God. This is part of the harmonious rhythm of the Mystical Body, whose Head is Christ and whose members are His chosen people.